Ca$hing in on
Credit Card$

Ca$hing in on Credit Card$

Making Money by Paying Your Bills

Scott A. Wheeler RT (R) (MR) (CT)

Order this book online at www.trafford.com
or email orders@trafford.com

Most Trafford titles are also available at major online book retailers.

Printed in the United States of America.

ISBN: 978-1-4669-0809-3 (sc)
ISBN: 978-1-4669-0810-9 (hc)
ISBN: 978-1-4669-0811-6 (e)

Library of Congress Control Number: 2012900686

Trafford rev. 01/19/2012

 www.trafford.com

North America & international
toll-free: 1 888 232 4444 (USA & Canada)
phone: 250 383 6864 ♦ fax: 812 355 4082

Special thanks to the credit card companies for all of the money.

CONTENTS

PREFACE

I hope you enjoy reading this book and find it useful.

My wife, Regina, and I made the decision to be a single-income family after the birth of our first son. Like most families, we struggled at times to make ends meet. We would try to find ways to earn extra income without cutting into our family time. For example, in the 1990s, we switched long-distance phone carriers every couple of months. We would cash checks for $50, $100, and $150 each time we made a switch.

Early in our marriage, we learned (the hard way) that only one person in the family should handle the finances; but even though one person writes the checks and balances the checkbook, there must always be an equal conversation and input about expenditures. Both spouses need to know what is going on with the finances.

Throughout the years we have used credit cards for extra cash and perks. It is nice to earn extra money by just paying your bills.

All of the stories in this book are fictional and do not represent any one person or situation; however, they are based loosely on similar situations that my wife and I have been through.

Thank you for reading.

CHAPTER 1

The Basics

Credit card offers. You get them in the mail. They seem to come every other day. The offers come in plain white envelopes or in highly decorated, eye-catching ones.

Companies promise $50, $100, $300, or more as sign-up bonuses for opening new credit card accounts. Often these promises come with other offers as well, like a 1 percent cash-back bonus on all purchases or 0 percent financing for a certain number of months.

The average person throws these mailings away without reading the contents. They usually call it all junk mail—but they are missing opportunities to make some money. All it takes is a little time and effort.

In this information age, the use of checks for paying bills is becoming obsolete. People across the globe are increasingly going online to pay their monthly bills and expenses with their debit cards. At the stores, the debit card is replacing cash.

The banks pay you nothing for using their debit cards. Some banks offer rewards programs. You usually have to pay to be in these rewards program, though; and the programs are not usually as lucrative as credit card companies' reward programs.

Your bank charges each merchant a fee whenever you use your debit card, but the bank usually does not let you in on the deal.

If a debit card offers no monetary return for its use, then why use it?

If a credit card company offers money back with every purchase or bill paid with it, why not use the credit card and become richer?

The most common cash-back bonus is usually a 1 percent cash-back bonus on all charges. This means, if you charge $5,000 in bills and expenses to your credit card, the credit card company will give you a fifty-dollar cash bonus.

This bonus may be applied to your balance, or it may be sent to you as a check or credited to your checking account. Sometimes the bonus can be converted to gift cards.

Some credit card companies offer special promotions such as 5 percent cash back on certain items for a certain length of time. This usually comes with a purchase limit.

A common example is the purchase of gasoline. The offer might be a 5 percent cash-back bonus on all gasoline purchases made from January to April. The maximum purchase amount qualifying for the 5 percent cash-back bonus might be $500.

If, for example, a credit card user purchases $800 worth of gas during the four months of this offer, he will earn a 5 percent cash-back bonus on the first $500 spent, which equals twenty-five dollars. The other $300 that the user charges will earn the customary 1 percent, which equals three dollars.

So for those four months, this person earns twenty-eight dollars for using his credit card to pay for his gas. He *always* pays off his credit card in full to avoid finance charges. Using his debit card to pay for his gas, on the other had, would earn him nothing.

Gasoline purchases are just one example. The credit card companies offer these types of deals on a variety of items. Credit card companies offer promotions on a variety of items and expenses including hotel stays, airline tickets, car rentals, clothes, shoes, home improvements, vitamins, lawn and garden supplies, and more.

The other type of bonus that credit card companies offer is the sign-up bonus. These sign-up bonuses can be $25, $50, $100, $150,

$300, or more. Sometimes the sign-up bonuses come in the form of gift cards. These are legitimate offers and are easy to obtain.

Some credit cards companies will offer the sign-up bonus after the first purchase. In this case, the user only needs to make a one small purchase. Two or three days later (which allows enough time for the purchase to post to his account), the user should go to the credit card's website and pay his account online from his checking account.

Companies will either automatically send a check after the first qualifying purchase or will post the balance on the next month's billing statement. The user can request to have the check mailed or to have the bonus credited to his checking account. If there is still a balance on the account, the bonus can be used to reduce or pay off the balance.

Instead of cash, some credit card companies offer gift cards, and the gift cards usually come with a bonus also. For example, if the initial bonus was for fifty dollars, the user may be able to get a sixty-dollar gift card instead of a fifty-dollar check. This is a way for the credit card user to earn even more.

Some credit card companies require a minimum purchase amount (for example, $250, $500, $1000, or more) to qualify for the sign-up bonus.

Large amounts such as $1,000 can be easily achieved by paying your bills with your credit card for a month. Of course, you *must* pay off your credit card in full so as not to incur any finance charges.

After making the qualifying amount of purchases, request the initial bonus as a check, account transfer, or gift card.

If, after receiving your initial bonus, you do not want to continue to have the credit card, feel free to cancel it.

I espouse four rules in this book:
1. Never pay any interest.
2. Never apply for a credit card with an annual fee.
3. Never pay a balance-transfer fee.
4. Have the money first; then charge the card, and pay it off.

The rest of this book is broken down into stories to illustrate these four principles. It starts simply with how to get your sign-up bonus and then moves on to how to cash in the cash-back bonus. It goes on to explain how to use 0 percent financing to make even more money, and how to transfer a balance without incurring a balance-transfer fee.

Chapter 2

Ralph Buys a Wireless Computer Router

In this chapter, you will learn how to qualify for a sign-up bonus after a single purchase and receive the bonus check in the mail.

Ralph is a thirty-something-year-old cheapskate. He is always on the lookout for a bargain. He always pays cash for any items he wants or needs, and he is not afraid to ask for a cash discount at the checkout counter.

Ralph has excellent credit. He pays all of his bills on time. If there is a discount for paying any of his bills ahead of time, he does it.

The credit card offers come almost every day to Ralph's household. He tears the envelopes in half and throws them in the trash. He considers these offers to be junk mail. They are not worthy of his time.

One day, Ralph and the family leave for a two-week vacation. The mail piles up, and after the family returns, as Ralph is sorting through the mail, he notices two credit card offers from the same company. One is addressed to his wife, Susan. This credit card offer promotes a hundred-dollar bonus after the first qualifying purchase.

The other envelope from the same company is addressed to Ralph. The enclosed letter offers a fifty-dollar bonus after the first qualifying purchase. This upsets Ralph. He—not Susan—is the one who pays the bills and balances the checkbook, and he makes more money; yet he gets offered less than his wife. He shoves both offers into the shredder.

Around two to three weeks later, the same credit card company sends out another credit card offer to Ralph. This time the offer is a $150 bonus after the first qualifying purchase. Ralph does not tear up or shred this envelope.

Ralph wants to get a wireless computer router for the household; it would make life more convenient. The router costs about $120 at the local computer outlet. That $150 bonus would pay for the router, and he would even have extra cash left over.

Ralph opens the envelope. At first, it seems too good to be true. Ralph reads all the paperwork that comes with the offer. He makes sure he understands it before he sends away for the credit card.

The credit card comes with a 1 percent cash-back bonus on all purchases, and it comes with 0 percent financing for nine months. These things do not matter to Ralph, though. It is the sign-up bonus of $150 that Ralph is interested in.

The initial purchase can be for any amount. That is all there is to it. Also, there is no annual fee. Ralph would never own a credit card with an annual fee.

He fills out the application. He signs the application. He mails the application.

He files all the paperwork that came with the credit card offer. If the company tries to pull a fast one on him, he will produce the paperwork and demand his money. Ralph does not like to be taken advantage of.

About ten days later, Ralph's shiny new credit card arrives in the mail. He opens the envelope and takes out the card. He calls the company's toll-free number to activate the card, and then he signs the back of the card in the signature area.

On his way to work the next day, Ralph stops at the local convenience store to gas up his vehicle. He decides to use his new credit card. He only charges twenty dollars because he does not feel comfortable using the new card. He still has doubts about the legitimacy of the offer.

He waits about a week to make sure the charges to the credit card have posted to his account. He goes online to the credit card company's website. He sets up a username and password. He sets up his checking account to pay for the credit card and then pays the entire balance (twenty dollars).

He does not use the credit card anymore.

About three to four weeks later, a check for $150 from the credit card company arrives.

The next day, on his way home from work, he deposits the check into his checking account.

The check posts to his account three days later. Ralph wastes no time. He calls the credit card company and cancels the credit card.

Ralph then cuts up his credit card into little pieces.

On his day off, Ralph goes to the local computer outlet and buys his $120 wireless computer router. He spends another ten dollars on computer paper. Of course, he has to ask the teenager next door (Jimmy) to help him set up the router. That cost Ralph the last twenty dollars—a tip for Jimmy.

Summary

Ralph learned how to make an easy $150. He now pays attention to these credit card offers coming in the mail. If the sign-up bonus is big enough for Ralph, he takes the plunge and applies for a new credit card. He follows this process for every credit card he applies for:

1. Receive a credit card offer in the mail. (This offer contains an initial bonus after charging a certain amount.)
2. Read the entire offer.
3. Make sure there is no annual fee.
4. Mail in the completed and signed application.

5. Receive the new credit card in mail.
6. Call the credit card company to activate the credit card.
7. Use the credit card enough to qualify for the bonus.
8. Pay off the credit card entirely.
9. Request the bonus.
10. Receive the bonus.
11. Call the credit card company and cancel the card.
12. Cut up the credit card.

Ralph has found out how easy it is to make a few extra dollars without a big time commitment. Ralph is proud of himself.

CHAPTER 3

Susan One-Ups Ralph

In this chapter, you will learn how to qualify for a sign-up bonus after charging a certain amount of money on a credit card. You will also learn how to request the sign-up bonus and have the bonus check mailed to the house.

Susan is married to Ralph from chapter two. She is a little upset at Ralph. She is happy he got his computer router for free, but she likes to be kept abreast of the finances.

Susan keeps an eye on the mail. She is on the lookout for her own credit card offer—with a bigger bonus than the one Ralph received. She has a competitive spirit.

The offer she has been waiting for arrives in the mail. The offer comes from the same company from which Ralph received his bonus money. The initial bonus offer is bigger than Ralph's bonus offer. This credit card offer comes with a $250 sign-up bonus after $1,000 in qualifying purchases. It also comes with a 1 percent cash-back bonus and 0 percent financing for nine months, but Susan is not interested in those two aspects. She only wants the sign-up bonus.

Susan reads the entire offer. She wants to understand what she is signing up for, and she wants to know the specifics regarding earning the sign-up bonus. No annual fee is involved. The offer looks good to Susan. After completing the application entirely, she signs it and puts the offer in the mail. Susan and Ralph have great credit scores. She is not worried about being turned down. She wants the credit card right away to start working toward her $250 sign-up bonus.

It takes about two weeks, but the shiny, new credit card with a sticker on the front of it finally arrives. She calls the telephone number on the sticker to activate her credit card.

The credit card company offers Susan credit protection and other products. Susan declines these offers. Her credit card is now ready for action.

Susan's plan is simple. Every two weeks, Ralph, who handles the finances, allots $600 to Susan from the couple's account for groceries, gas, and incidentals. Instead of paying cash for these expenses, she is going to use her credit card. She plans to pay off the credit card with the cash she was going to use for those expenses.

The next day is payday. Susan withdraws the usual $600 from their checking account at the local bank ATM. She tucks the money away in a secret pouch in her Coach purse. She is keeping her plans secret from Ralph. She wants to surprise him.

For the next two weeks, she uses her new credit card at the local grocery store, gas station, convenience store, coffee shop, department store, and discount shop. She keeps every receipt and writes down the amounts on a note pad; this way she can keep track of her expenses and stay within her budget. She charges $590 on her credit card.

Two weeks later, Susan again withdraws her biweekly $600 from the checking account.

This time Susan charges $580 on her credit card during the two-week period between paydays. The total balance on her credit card is now $1,170.

Susan deposits $1,170 in cash back into her checking account. She is relieved, as she did not like carrying around over a thousand dollars in her purse.

At home, she goes online to the credit card company's website. She sets up her username and her password. She sets up her method of payment; the credit card will be paid with her checking account. She pays off the credit card completely.

She looks in the bonus section of the online statement, but the box reads $0. It sometimes takes a couple of weeks for a credit card company to record the bonus. Susan logs off the website.

One week later, Susan logs on to the credit card company's website again. This time there is a number in her bonus account. She has earned $261.70. $250 is her sign-up bonus for making over $1,000 in charges. The other $11.70 is the 1 percent cash-back bonus she earned on $1,170 in charges.

Susan cannot take the whole $261.70 right away, though. The bonus is only redeemable in increments of fifty dollars. Susan requests that a $250 check be mailed to her home. She logs off the website.

The check arrives in the mail about a week later. Susan drives to the bank and cashes it immediately, receiving two one-hundred-dollar bills and a fifty-dollar bill.

When she gets back home, she puts the money on the kitchen table. This is so Ralph can see it when he gets home.

Ralph comes home. He sees the money on the table and asks, "What's up with the cash?"

"Remember how you made $150 for the computer router?" asks Susan.

"Yeah," Ralph says hesitantly.

"Well, I did the same thing. I got a new credit card, but I got a $250 sign-up bonus. Isn't that great?" exclaims Susan. She takes the money off the table and puts it her purse.

Ralph shakes his head. He just got schooled. They both have a good laugh.

They now work on cashing in on credit cards together.

Summary

Susan has learned how easy it is to make some extra money by paying her expenses with a credit card using the same steps Bill took.

1. Receive a credit card offer in the mail. (This offer contains an initial bonus after charging a certain amount.)
2. Read the entire offer.
3. Make sure there is no annual fee.
4. Mail in the completed and signed application.
5. Receive the new credit card in mail.
6. Call the credit card company to activate the credit card.
7. Use the credit card enough to qualify for the bonus.
8. Pay off the credit card entirely.
9. Request the bonus.
10. Receive the bonus.
11. Call the credit card company and cancel the card.
12. Cut up the credit card.

Susan and Ralph now work together like a married couple should. The most Ralph and Susan have made in one month is $850.

Ralph and Susan would like to leave you with one last tip for married couples. Apply for a credit card in one spouse's name only. This way the credit card company may offer one spouse a bonus; then later the same company may offer the other spouse a bonus. If they apply together for a credit card, they may only be eligible for one bonus instead of two.

Chapter 4

Bill Buys a Fly-Fishing Rod

In this chapter, you will learn how to qualify for multiple sign-up bonuses to achieve a certain goal. You will also learn how to credit your checking account with these sign-up bonuses.

Bill is your typical middle-aged guy. He stands around six feet tall, and he weighs in at about 250 pounds. He enjoys life. His favorite pastime is fishing. Fly-fishing for trout is his ultimate getaway from the everyday pressures of life. A bumper sticker on the back of his truck reads, "I'd rather be fishing."

Bill likes having all the special fly-fishing gear. He has the best reel, line, leader, and a wide of assortment of flies. According to Bill, he only lacks that one special lightweight fly rod.

Money has been tight since his wife was laid off. Bill just can't go out and spend $300 on the fly-fishing rod of his dreams.

One day Bill is in his favorite sporting goods store checking out the latest fishing gear. At this store, which sells the $300 fly-fishing rod he wants, Bill sees an advertisement for the company's credit card.

The credit card offers a twenty-five-dollar gift card to the department store with $250 in charges. Bill does not ask his wife about applying for the credit card. He figures she would not approve of the situation. She does not like having any debts, especially since losing her job.

Bill's credit card application is accepted, and he uses the card to fill up his big blue pick-up truck for the next couple of weeks. He charges about $265. He goes online to the credit card's website and pays off the card immediately. He requests the twenty-five-dollar gift card from the credit card's website.

The twenty-five-dollar gift card arrives in the mail several days later. Bill then cancels his credit card. He cuts it up and throws it in the trash.

He shows his wife the gift card. Then he gets up the courage to ask his wife, "Can I buy a new fly-fishing rod with this twenty-five dollars?"

Bill's wife asks how he got the gift card, and she is not happy when she finds out. She is mad at Bill for not telling her about opening a credit card account. She asks, "How much is the rod you want?"

"Three hundred dollars," Bill replies with a lump in his throat.

"Well," she says, "You have twenty-five dollars, but you still need to come up with $275 plus spending money."

Bill is not frazzled.

Bill takes out his wallet. He pulls out a new credit card. "With this card, I will earn one hundred dollars after I charge $1,000."

"What are you going to buy for $1,000?" she snaps at Bill.

"It's okay. It's okay. I am just going to pay the usual bills and gas up the vehicles with this charge card. I have the money to pay these bills now. But first I am going to pay them with this credit card. Then I will pay off the credit card right away." Bill continues, "Then I'll collect the one-hundred-dollar bonus and close the account. I promise."

"That's fine. I leave this in your hands. Don't mess it up," his wife responds. She is not happy, but Bill has always handled the finances. She knows he will handle it the right way.

Bill has also received two other offers from credit card companies, but he has not yet sent away for them. He wanted to have this conversation with his wife first. Now that they've talked, he sends the applications in to be approved.

Bill pays his bills and puts gasoline in both vehicles using his credit card. He gets his total a little over $1,000.

Three days later, Bill goes online to the credit card's website and pays off the entire balance.

Two weeks later, he requests his one-hundred-dollar sign-up bonus. He has the bonus deposited directly to his checking account.

Two days later, the one hundred dollars is credited to his checking account. He calls the credit card company, cancels his credit card, and then cuts it up.

Bill's two new credit cards arrive in the mail.

One card comes with a fifty-dollar initial bonus after charging $500.

The other card comes with a $150 initial bonus after the first purchase. There is no purchase threshold for this card. Bill uses this card first.

On his way home from work one day, Bill stops at the local convenience store and purchases a gallon of milk. He uses the $150-bonus credit card to make the purchase.

During the next two weeks, Bill pays some bills and puts gasoline in both vehicles using the credit card with the fifty-dollar initial bonus. He charges about $600.

Two days later, Bill goes online and pays off both credit cards entirely. He never carries a balance. This would make his wife unhappy.

Bill also asks his wife to fill out a credit card application that comes in the mail for her. Well, in reality Bill fills it out and just asks his wife to sign it. With a little coaxing from her husband of over twenty years, she signs the application. Bill mails it in.

The next day Bill receives a $150 check as a sign-up bonus from one credit card company. Bill is happily surprised that he did not have to make a request online. He deposits the check into his checking account. Bill has now received $250 and a twenty-five-dollar gift card.

He immediately goes online to request the fifty-dollar bonus from the other credit card company. The company deposits the bonus into his checking account in about three days. He has now received a total of $300 and a twenty-five-dollar gift card. He has enough for the fly-fishing rod, but he needs gas and food money to get to his fishing hole.

Bill's wife's credit card arrives in the mail. On her application, Bill had requested a card in his name. This way Bill can use the card, and the wife will have no headaches. Bill tries to keep life simple.

This card offers a fifty-dollar sign-up bonus after the user charges $500.

Bill immediately puts it to use buying the groceries (the wife says that's a first) and putting gasoline in the vehicles. He is getting excited about the upcoming fishing trip he is now planning. He charges about $525 on the card.

He has also received another credit card application for his wife. He fills it out and has the wife sign the application.

Three days later Bill pays off the credit card with the $525 balance. He checks the bonus statement area on the credit card's website, but there is no bonus credited yet. Bill knows by now that it can sometimes take up to two weeks or more for a bonus to be credited to his account. He is just excited.

Two weeks later a fifty-dollar check from the credit card company arrives in the mail. He immediately deposits the check into his checking account. He has now received $350 and a twenty-five-dollar gift card.

After the check clears, Bill has his wife cancel the credit card. This she does happily!

The next day, the wife's new credit card arrives along with one for Bill also. She calls the credit card company to activate her card. This does not make her happy. Bill promises her that this will be the last one.

This credit card comes with a one-hundred-dollar initial bonus after $1,000 in charges.

Bill immediately charges all the bills, buys the groceries (his wife is ecstatic but surprised by some of the items) and puts gasoline in both vehicles. He gets to the $1,000 level in no time. Three days later, he goes onto the credit card's website and fully pays off the balance. He knows what he'll find, but he checks anyway. The bonus has not been credited to his account yet.

Every day for three weeks, Bill goes online to see if the hundred-dollar bonus has posted to his account. He calls the credit card company. He asks an employee of the credit card company how much longer it will be before the bonus is credited to his account. The operator says the company can credit the account that very day. This makes Bill happy. He has the bonus sent to his checking account.

Two days later the one-hundred-dollar bonus appears in Bill's checking account. He has the wife call the credit card company and cancel the card. He has now received a total of $450 and a twenty-five-dollar gift card since his endeavor began.

Bill finally buys his $300 fly-fishing rod. It cost Bill nothing. In fact, he now has an extra $150. He buys some extra leader and a couple of brightly colored flies. The rest he will use for gas and food.

Bill makes it to his favorite fishing hole, a spot on an ice-cold, fast-flowing, clear river. It is a bright, clear day. There are only a few clouds in the beautiful blue sky. It is seventy-six degrees with just a slight breeze—a perfect day for fishing.

Bill puts on his waders and moves into the river. He scans up and down the river for where the trout may be hiding. For over two hours he moves up and down the river, casting and searching for that one area where the prize is lurking. Cast after cast produces nothing, not a bite or a splash. He sees no fish.

He then sees an unusual swirl in a tiny pool across the river. It looks like the perfect spot, but in the middle of the river the current is too strong.

But Bill has just bought the ultimate lightweight fly-fishing rod. He tries to cast his fly into the pool. He misses several times, but the last time he tries it makes it there.

As soon as the reddish-brown fly hits the water, a monster of a fish comes from below the surface and gulps it up.

Bill's pole bends in half immediately. He sets the hook. The fight is on!

An exhausting fight is given for both fish and fisherman. The tug-of-war and give-and-take last around fifteen minutes. Bill finally gets the rainbow trout close enough to him. He nets the gigantic, rainbow-colored, exhausted fish.

This is Bill's biggest rainbow trout. It is the biggest fresh water fish that Bill has ever caught.

He carries the trophy fish and his equipment back up the river to his truck. He immediately takes out the fish scale. The trout weighs in at thirteen pounds and three ounces. He ices the trout right away.

Bill quickly stores all of his gear in the pick-up. He is excited. He takes out his navigation system and looks up the nearest taxidermist.

He exceeds the speed limits to get to the taxidermist. He hands his prize over to the lady behind the counter, but not until the lady uses his digital camera to take several pictures of Bill and the rainbow trout. He wants the pictures to prove to his friends and family the fish story he is going to relate to everybody.

When Bill arrives back home, he pulls his pick-up into his driveway and bangs on the horn several times.

The wife peers out the front window. She is surprised that Bill is back so soon. She rushes out to see what is wrong.

Bill is all smiles. He shows his wife the pictures of the trout. Bill tells her, "I could not have done it without this new fly-fishing rod."

She just rolls her eyes. "Where's the fish?" she asks.

"Oh, I am getting it stuffed and mounted. It is going to look great in the den."

She rolls her eyes again. A fish mounted on the wall in her house would not fit in with her décor.

"How much did it cost?" she asks.

"A little under a hundred dollars," Bill replies.

"How are you going to pay for it?" she asks.

"Don't worry—I'll find a way," Bill says.

The wife sighs.

Six weeks later Bill hands his wife a one-hundred-dollar bill. This is payment for the mounted rainbow trout he caught with his new fly-fishing rod.

He received the hundred dollars from a new credit card offer— and, yes, he pays the balance, cancels the credit card, and cuts it up.

Summary

Bill earned $450 in cash and a twenty-five-dollar gift card to his favorite store. These were the steps Bill took to accomplish his goals.

1. Receive a credit card offer in the mail. (This offer contains an initial bonus after charging a certain amount.)
2. Read the entire offer.
3. Make sure there is no annual fee.
4. Mail in the completed and signed application.
5. Receive the new credit card in mail.
6. Call the credit card company to activate the credit card.
7. Use the credit card enough to qualify for the bonus.
8. Pay off the credit card entirely.
9. Request the bonus.
10. Receive the bonus.
11. Call the credit card company and cancel the card.
12. Cut up the credit card.
13. Repeat until goal is met.

Chapter 5

Henry Bets on Football

In this chapter, you will learn how to get paid for paying your monthly expenses with your credit card by using the cash-back bonuses that credit card companies offer.

Henry is a gentleman in his mid-sixties. For over thirty years, he paid all of his bills through the mail with checks. It has been a slow evolution over the last ten years, but Henry eventually achieved proficiency in using his checking account to pay bills online.

Henry is thrilled about not having to purchase boxes of checks. Checking is now practically free. One box of checks can last over a year in today's information age.

But Henry has been wondering. The bank makes money every time he makes a debit card purchase. The bank charges the merchant, but Henry is not in on the action. Henry wants in on the action.

Henry's credit card company keeps claiming that it offers a 1 percent cash-back bonus on all purchases. The company advertises this on TV and on the monthly statements Henry receives after those rare occasions when he uses his credit card. Henry figures he would use his credit card to pay his bills online if that would count toward the 1 percent cash-back bonus. He decides to call the credit card company to find out.

The credit card company answers yes. Henry is thrilled. The young lady from the company also lets Henry know that he'll be able to cash in his cash-back bonuses in increments of fifty dollars.

The bank never pays Henry to pay his bills. The bank does have a rewards program for its debit card; but signing up would cost money up front to sign up, and the card comes with an annual fee. The bank offers an online bill-paying service, but it charges for that service as well.

Henry decides to use his credit card to pay his bills online. Henry wants to get paid for doing this thankless chore. For every $5,000 he pays in bills, he will make fifty dollars. "This is a better deal than using the bank," Henry reasons to himself.

A couple of days later, the monthly cable bill arrives in the mail. Henry laments, "TV used to be free." (He says this every month.)

He goes online to pay the dreaded cable bill. Instead of using his checking account information, Henry clicks the "add on a new payment account" button on the cable company's website. He puts in his new credit card information and pays the cable bill with his credit card. It was not difficult or time consuming for Henry.

Three days later, Henry logs on to the credit card company's website. He sees that the new balance from the cable bill has posted to his account. He pays the credit card off using his checking account. He always pays off his credit card balances entirely. It would be pointless to try to acquire a cash-back bonus if he were to carry a balance; it would be a losing situation.

Henry's rent and homeowners association fee are due on the first of the month. Henry calls the cable company, cell phone company, gas company, electric company, water company, and the insurance company. He has all of his bills adjusted so that payments are due on the first of the month. This way Henry only needs to charge his bills once a month.

For the next four months, Henry pays all of his bills with his credit card on the thirtieth of each month. On the seventh of each month, Henry pays off the entire balance of his credit card. He waits until the seventh of the month so that all of his charges will be posted to his credit card account. This way there will be no detrimental finance charges.

During these four months, Henry charges $8,000 on his credit card. This earns Henry eighty dollars in his cash-back bonus account.

He cannot take the entire eighty dollars out because the cash-back bonus must be taken in increments of fifty dollars. Henry goes online to the credit card company's website and requests a direct deposit into his checking account for fifty dollars of his cash-back bonus.

It takes about two or three days for the fifty dollars to post to Henry's checking account. Henry is elated at how easy it is to earn a few dollars by just paying your bills with a credit card.

Henry pays his bills like this for a year. He cashes in $300 for just paying his bills.

Football season is drawing near. Henry likes to bet on college football. "Just having five dollars on a game, makes the game so much more interesting," he says. (This is Henry's excuse for wagering.)

He visits the local casino, which offers online sports wagering. He fills out the application for his online gambling account and turns over the $300 he has earned by paying his bills. The sports book gives Henry a complimentary prime rib dinner at the café in the casino. This is his favorite food. Henry considers the dinner an added bonus for using the credit card to pay his bills.

Don't let Henry fool you. He knows what he is doing betting on football. He ends the college football season ahead another 75 percent; in other words, Henry has made another $250 betting on college football teams. He does not credit the credit card company for his $250 in winnings. That Henry takes the credit for.

Summary

This is how Henry earned $300 in a year.

His rent and homeowner's association fee were due the first of the month. He called up the companies that sent him regular monthly bills and had all their due dates changed to the first of the month. He paid all the bills with his credit card on the thirtieth of every month. On the seventh of the month, he paid off the credit card entirely from his checking account.

Instead of using his checking account to pay his bills, Henry uses his credit card to pay his bills. Then he pays off the credit card. This way Henry gets paid for paying his bills.

Pretty smart of Henry, isn't it?

Chapter 6

Christy Buys New Shoes

In this chapter, you will learn how to make money off the sign-up bonuses and cash-back bonuses by cashing in your rewards for gift cards of greater value.

Christy is your typical second-year college student. Money is always tight, so she is always looking for a way to save or earn an easy dollar.

Tuition and books are not a problem for Christy. Her parents have contributed to a 529 college savings plan since before she was born. Christy wishes she could dip into this money for the little extras in life. For Christy, this means buying new shoes!

The upcoming semester is her third semester. She knows the routine. Her dad calls the brokerage firm and initiates a $5,200 withdrawal for the semester. He then forwards the funds to Christy. She uses the money to pay for her tuition and books.

Christy has been paying her own bills for the past year. She has not missed a payment, and she has not been late on any bills.

Two months before the fall semester, Christy applies for a credit card. She has never owned a credit card before. The credit card advertises a one-hundred-dollar sign-up bonus after $1,000 in purchases. This is a tempting offer to a cash-strapped college student.

Christy receives the credit card in the mail two weeks later. The credit card comes with a $6,500 limit. Besides the hundred-dollar sign-up bonus, the card offers 1 percent cash back on all purchases. The cash-back bonuses can be taken in fifty-dollar increments or in twenty-five-dollar gift cards.

Christy calls the credit card company and activates the card immediately. Then she visits the credit card company's website and sets up her online account.

Around the middle of August, Dad's $5,200 shows up in Christy's checking account.

Christy pays for her fall semester tuition and her books with her credit card.

Two days later, she accesses her credit card statement online and sees the $5,200 balance. She sets up her method of payment for the card (her checking account) and then pays off the $5,200 from her checking account. She looks into the bonus area of her online statement, but nothing is in the bonus account.

Two weeks later the cash-back bonus shows up in her online account. She has earned $152 for paying her tuition and books with her new credit card. One hundred dollars was the sign-up bonus she earned after charging the first $1,000 on her credit card. The $52 came from her 1 percent cash-back bonus she earned on the total $5,200 she charged for her tuition and books.

The cash-back bonus can only be taken in increments of fifty dollars. She decides to cash out $150.

As she is about to request the check, she notices there are gift cards available to choose from. She can use her cash-back bonus to purchase gift cards to movies, department stores, specialty shops, shoe stores, and more. These gift cards cost twenty-five dollars, but they are worth thirty dollars. Her favorite shoe store is offering one of these thirty-dollar gift cards for twenty-five dollars. Shoe shopping is her weakness.

Christy decides on a one-hundred-dollar check and two thirty-dollar gift cards to her favorite shoe store. She buys a pair of red high heels. Red is her favorite color.

Summary

Christy earned $160 using her credit card to pay for her college expenses. Her dad is impressed—and he is not the easiest man to please. Christy is very proud of herself.

Christy repeats this scenario every semester. She receives a new credit card with a bonus after making so much in purchases. One semester Christy received a $300 bonus! Her dad now takes advantage of these offers too.

Christy has kept her original credit card all through college. She charges her everyday expenses and bills, and she pays off her balances immediately. About every three or four months, she requests two thirty-dollar gift cards and goes shoe shopping.

CHAPTER 7

Alice Pays for Bowling

In this chapter, you'll learn how to use a sign-up bonus, varying rates of cash-back bonuses, and an additional bonus to pay for a favorite pastime.

Alice is an avid bowler. She bowls on a league every year with three of her closest girlfriends. The name of their bowling team is the Lady Dragons. The Lady Dragons finished in second place last year.

Their second-place finish brought in enough money for each team member to buy a new and improved bowling ball for their upcoming season. This year, their goal is first place!

Alice finished last season with a bowling average of 166. With the new bowling ball, she hopes to improve her average to 170 or more! The bowling ball should provide more hook and power when it strikes the bowling pins.

The Lady Dragons' season usually begins on the first Wednesday after Labor Day, and the season ends around Mother's Day. The fall bowling season is thirty-two weeks long.

Alice pays for the entire bowling season and sanction fees on the first day of bowling. She earns the money for the bowling season during the prior year. She pays her bills and other expenses with a credit card that offers a sign-up bonus, a cash-back bonus, and a cashing-in bonus.

Alice's offer of interest comes in the mail at the end of May. This credit card offer comes with 0 percent financing for eighteen months. This does not interest Alice because Alice will always pay the balance off well ahead of schedule. Alice does not believe in paying interest. "I don't want to make anybody else rich—only myself," Alice says.

What strikes Alice's fancy this time are the bonuses offered with this credit card.

1. A hundred-dollar sign-up bonus after $500 in qualifying purchases
2. A 1 percent cash-back bonus on all purchases
3. Three percent cash back on groceries and gas for the first six months
4. Redeem $300 or more on cash-back bonuses and earn an additional 25 percent.
5. No annual fee
6. Bonuses can be taken in increments of twenty-five dollars.

Alice reads the entire credit card offer. She wants to make sure she understands the terms of the deal. Knowledge is power; ignorance costs money. She completes the entire application, and she mails the completed application off to the credit card company.

By the middle of June, Alice's new credit card arrives in the mail. When she calls to activate her credit card, the credit card company tries to offer Alice credit protection products, but she refuses these offers. "A waste of money," Alice says. She removes the sticker from the front of her new credit card, and she signs the back of the card.

Every month Alice has the following expenses:

Monthly Expenses

Gasoline	$400
Power, natural gas, and water	$400
Car insurance	$200
Groceries	$600
Cable	$150
Telephone (including cellular)	$150
Total	$1,900

This credit card offers a 3 percent cash-back bonus on groceries and gasoline for the first six months. Alice will earn thirty dollars a month for charging her gasoline and groceries on her credit card. She will earn an additional nine dollars (1 percent cash back) for paying her normal monthly bills with her credit card. For the first six months, Alice will earn thirty-nine dollars a month in cash-back bonuses.

Monthly Cash-Back Bonus Breakdown

Gasoline and groceries: $1,000 @ 3 percent $30
Power, natural gas, water, car insurance,
cable, and telephone bills: $900 @ 1 percent $ 9
Monthly bonus earned $39

Every three months, Alice and her husband have four other expenses which she will charge to her credit card. They are the sewer bill, garbage bill, life insurance premiums, and property taxes.

Expenses Incurred Every Three Months

Sewer	$ 60
Garbage	$ 40
Life Insurance	$200
Property Taxes	$600
Total	$900

Alice begins using her new credit card to pay her monthly expenses right away. She also immediately goes to the credit card company's website. She chooses her username and password and sets up her account to receive payments from her checking account. She will pay the entire balance off every week. Alice will never carry a balance forward since that would defeat the whole purpose of cashing in on credit cards. The credit card company will almost always charge you more in interest than it will pay you in bonuses.

In July, Alice charges all of her monthly expenses with her credit card. She charges $1,900 to her credit card. She pays off the entire balance. She earns thirty dollars for charging $1,000 in gasoline and groceries (3 percent for the first six months), and she earns nine dollars (1 percent) for charging $900 on all her other monthly bills.

July's cash-back balance is thirty-nine dollars.

In August, Alice charges the same amount, $1,900, to her credit card. She pays off the entire balance. She again earns another thirty-nine dollars as a cash-back bonus. Her credit card account is also credited the hundred-dollar sign-up bonus for Alice charging $500 to her account.

August's cash-back balance is $178.

In September, Alice charges the $1,900 to her credit card. Every three months, the sewer bill, garbage bill, the life insurance premiums, and the property taxes are due. She charges these bills to her credit card also. This is an additional $900. She pays off her balance completely. This month she earns forty-eight dollars. ($1,000 @ 3 percent equals thirty dollars, and $1,800 @ 1 percent equals eighteen dollars.)

September's cash-back balance is $226.

In October, Alice charges the usual monthly expenses of $1,900 to her credit card. She earns thirty-nine dollars for her cash-back bonus. She pays off the entire credit card balance.

October's cash-back balance is $265.

In November, Alice continues to use her credit card to pay for her monthly expenses. She charges $1,900 to her credit card, and she immediately pays off the entire balance. Alice again earns a thirty-nine-dollar cash-back bonus.

November's cash-back balance is $304.

In December, the Christmas shopping season arrives. Alice charges all of her Christmas shopping to her credit card. This comes to $1,000. She also charges her usual monthly expenses ($1,900) to her credit card, and she charges her usual three-month expenses ($900). This month, her total charges equal $3,800. She pays off the balance completely. She earns a cash-back bonus of fifty-eight dollars.

December's cash-back balance is $362.

In January, Alice charges her usual $1,900 to her credit card. The 3 percent cash back on gasoline and groceries expires. Now all purchases earn only 1 percent cash back. This month, Alice earns a cash-back bonus of nineteen dollars.

January's cash-back balance is $381.

February is the same as January. Alice charges $1,900 to her credit card, and she pays off the balance entirely. She earns a nineteen-dollar cash-back bonus.

February's cash-back balance is $400.

In March, the quarterly bills come due. She charges all of her expenses (a total of $2,800) to her credit card. She pays off the balance completely. She earns a cash-back bonus of twenty-eight dollars.

March's cash-back balance is $428.

In April, Alice charges $6,900 to her credit card. $1,900 is her usual monthly expenses; the other $5,000 goes to pay for a cruise to the Bahamas with her husband. She pays off the entire balance. This month, Alice earns a cash-back bonus of sixty-nine dollars.

April's cash-back balance is $497.

In May, Alice charges her usual $1,900 to her credit card. She pays off the credit card. She earns a nineteen-dollar cash-back bonus.

May's cash-back balance is $516.

It is time for Alice to cash in her bonus account. She logs on to the credit card company's website and goes to the bonus section of her online statement.

The cash-back bonus must be taken in increments of twenty-five dollars. She requests that $500 be transferred to her checking account.

She earns a 25 percent bonus on her cash-back bonus. (With this credit card, anytime an amount of $300 or more is redeemed as a cash-back bonus, an additional 25 percent cash bonus is credited to the account.)

Alice earns a 25 percent bonus on $400, not on the full $500 (because one hundred dollars was a sign-up bonus, which is not usually subject to the 25 percent bonus). Alice earns one hundred dollars on the $400 redeemed.

A deposit of $600 shows up in Alice's checking account about three days later. She earned $600 in eleven months by just paying her monthly bills and expenses.

During these last eleven months, Alice also earned an additional $250 in other credit cards.

Every year, around the beginning of fall, Alice and her husband receive credit card offers that offer sign-up bonuses with a single purchase.

In October Alice receives an offer for a credit card with a $150 sign-up bonus. There is no minimum purchase amount; only one qualifying purchase is needed. She signs up for the credit card and makes a small purchase after the card comes in the mail. Alice pays off the credit card. She receives her $150 check. She cancels the credit card and cuts it up.

Alice's husband receives an offer from the same company that sent Alice the $150. The company only offers him a hundred-dollar sign-up bonus. It is the same situation. There is not a qualifying purchase amount, and only one qualifying purchase is required. Alice has her husband sign up for the credit card. He makes a small purchase. A one-hundred-dollar check is mailed to their home. Alice deposits the check in the bank account. Alice pays off the credit card. Alice has her husband cancel the credit card. Alice cuts up the credit card.

Alice earns $850 for the bowling season.

$600 from original credit card
$150 from Alice's additional credit card
<u>$100</u> from Alice's husband's credit card
$850

Summary

Bowling fees for the week are fifteen dollars. There are thirty-two weeks of bowling plus thirty dollars in sanctions fees. The total cost for bowling fees for the year equals $510. After using her cash-bonus money to pay for bowling expenses, Alice has $340 left over.

At the end of last season when the Lady Dragons finished second, the ladies all bought new bowling balls to increase their averages. Alice's bowling ball increases her hook. This has made it harder for Alice to knock down the ten pin. (The ten pin is the bowling pin in the back on the right hand side of the bowling lane. This is a right-handed bowler's nightmare.) Alice has decided to buy a plastic bowling ball to smash that ten pin! (A plastic bowling ball usually does not have a hook. It is a straight ball.)

The Lady Dragons have made it to finals again this year. They are evenly matched with another team.

Now the whole season has come down to the tenth frame of the last game of the last bowler, Alice.

The Lady Dragons need ten pins to win the championship. Alice steps up onto the bowling lane. She grabs her bowling ball from the rack. She approaches the line. She is nervous. She takes a deep breath to calm her nerves.

She spies her mark on the lanes. She begins her approach. The ball is released perfectly from her hand. Her form is statuesque. The ball flows over the fifth board just as Alice hopes. The bowling ball comes up to the pocket. It is a loud, hard pocket shot. Alice and her teammates think she has the strike—but she doesn't. The ten pin in the right-hand corner is still standing by itself. The series is tied. Alice needs to pick up the ten pin.

Alice goes back to the bowling rack and takes her plastic bowling ball in hand. She says she's not nervous, but one of her teammates thinks she sees Alice's legs shake a little. Alice keeps her eye on the mark throughout her entire approach to line. The bowling ball rolls straight. It rolls straight into that blasted ten pin!

She has done it. The Lady Dragons win the season!

With their winnings, the ladies go to Las Vegas, and they have a great time!

And it is all paid for by the credit card companies.

Chapter 8

David Uses Credit Card Money to Make Money

In this chapter, you will learn how to make money off the credit card company's money.

David is a small business owner in his mid-forties. He is always on the lookout for a way to generate more income.

Because of his business, he usually receives more credit card offers in the mail than most people. He discards the offers because he considers them junk mail.

One day a highly decorated envelope catches David's eye. It is from a credit card company offering a $150 sign-up bonus after the first qualifying purchase.

He opens the envelope, thinking it will end up being a waste of time. He reads the introduction letter. It sounds good. He then reads the entire offer. He wants to understand the whole process. He does not want to be taken advantage of.

He makes sure that there is no annual fee for the card. David would never pay an annual fee. That would be a waste of money.

The offer appears legitimate to David. All he needs to do is make one purchase, and then the credit card company will send David a $150 check in the mail or credit his account balance with $150.

David wants to confirm the details of the agreement on the sign-up bonus with a human being from the credit card company. David calls the toll-free number on the letter.

The representative from the credit card company confirms the details of the offer to David. The representative asks David if he would like to complete the credit card offer over the phone, and David agrees to do this. He knows it will speed up the process.

He gives the representative his full name, social security number, date of birth, home and cell phone numbers, annual income, mortgage payment amount, and e-mail address.

A couple of minutes later, the representative tells David his application has been accepted. She lets him know what his credit limit will be. She also tells David that he will receive the credit card in about seven days.

Less than seven days later, the credit card arrives in the mail. David calls the telephone number on the sticker on the front of the credit card to activate the card. The representative from the credit card company tries to talk David into signing up for credit protection services. David declines; it would be a waste of money.

David's credit card comes with a 1 percent cash-back bonus on all purchases, but during the months of January through March, his credit card offers a 5 percent cash-back bonus on gasoline, airline, and hotel purchases. He must go the company's website to sign up for the 5 percent cash-back bonus. There is a limit to the amount he can charge to receive the 5 percent cash-back bonus. He can only spend $1,500 and receive the 5 percent cash-back bonus. Any gasoline, airline, or hotel purchases made above the first $1,500 would only receive the customary 1 percent cash back.

David goes to the credit card company's website. He sets up his account. He chooses his username and password. He signs up for the 5 percent cash back on gasoline, airline, and hotel purchases.

David has his own car, his wife's car, and the company's three trucks. For the next two to three weeks, David uses the credit card to fuel up the vehicles. He gets to the $1,500 in no time. In fact, he charges $1,800 to the credit card. He immediately pays off the balance. The credit card comes with 0 percent financing for twelve months, but David just wants to use the credit card to make a few extra bucks.

David checks the credit card statement online for the next few weeks to see if his bonuses have appeared in his account yet. Every time he checks, he is disappointed.

It takes about seven weeks. The bonus appears on his online statement. In the bonus section of his statement, David sees that he has earned $228. He clicks on the button labeled "request check."

He enters the amount he wants to redeem ($228). This produces an error. David is told he can only take the bonus in increments of twenty-five dollars. David redeems $225.

David's $225 check arrives in the mail seven days later. "Easy money," he says to himself.

David drives to the bank and deposits the check into his savings account. He wants to try to earn a little interest on other people's money.

After the check clears, David calls the credit card company to cancel the credit card. The company representative asks David why. He tells them, "I took advantage of the credit card offer for the $150 sign-up bonus. And I also took advantage of the 5 percent cash back for gas purchases. I have been very happy with your company and your people. I just don't need the card anymore."

The representative responds, "Thank you for your honesty. We find you to be a valuable customer. We do not want to lose your business. We are prepared to offer you another fifty-dollar bonus if you charge an additional $1,500 to your credit card. Would you be interested in staying with us and taking advantage of this offer?"

David does not take long to reply. He agrees to stay with the credit card company.

David is now going to use the credit card for all of his business expenses. He will pay off the balance immediately. He wants to cash in on the 1 percent cash-back bonus.

David receives an offer from a bank he does not do business with. This bank's deal offers a hundred-dollar sign-up bonus for opening a free checking account. The minimum deposit is one hundred dollars, and the checking account must remain open for 180 days.

The next day, David goes to his bank's ATM and withdraws one hundred dollars from his savings account. In his mind, David is using the credit card company's one hundred dollars to make more money.

He drives over to the other bank. He signs up for the free checking account the bank offered him that comes with the hundred-dollar bonus. He is told that his one hundred dollars will show up in his account in two to three weeks.

Two weeks later, the hundred-dollar bonus shows up in David's checking account. He is elated at how easy it is to make a few extra bucks here or there. He does not know why he has not been doing this for years.

Two weeks later, the same bank that offered David the one-hundred-dollar bonus for opening the checking account sends David another offer for a one-hundred-dollar bonus. To receive this bonus, David must open a savings account with a $5,000 balance, and he must maintain that $5,000 balance for six months.

This is no problem for David. For the past month, David has been using his credit card for all of his business expenses in order to earn the 1 percent cash-back bonus. He charges $6,000 in business expenses on his credit card. He takes the $5,000 he would have used to pay off the credit card and opens a savings account at the bank offering the sign-up bonus. He sends in the other $1,000 to the credit card company as his monthly payment.

For the next six months, David will charge about $6,000 in business expenses to his credit card. He will also send in a $6,000 monthly payment to the credit card company. He will carry a balance of $5,000 on his credit card. He has 0 percent financing for six months. During those six months, he will earn 1 percent annual interest on the $5,000 in the savings account.

After the six-month qualifying period for the savings account is over, David goes back to the bank. He closes both the checking and savings accounts. He waits for the savings account's qualifying period to end before he closes the checking account. This saves David gasoline money and time.

David earns twenty-five dollars in interest from the savings account. (David has now earned $450 by using a credit card. He has cashed in $225 in bonuses, $100 from opening a checking account, $100 from opening a savings account, and $25 in interest.)

He takes the $5,000 and sends it in as a payment for the credit card. David continues to charge his $6,000 in business expenses to his credit card for the next four months, and he pays the balance entirely each month.

At the end of the four months, David stops using the credit card. He does not have a balance. He decides not to use the credit card because the 0 percent financing has ended. He does not want to run the risk of carrying a balance and end up paying interest charges. This would be detrimental to his business and his person.

During these past ten months, David has charged $60,000 to his credit card, earning $600 in 1 percent cash-back bonuses. He also earns the fifty-dollar retention bonus, the credit card company offered him to stay with the company.

David goes to the credit card company's website. He requests that a $650 check be mailed to his home. The check arrives in seven days. He deposits the check into his original savings account. He wants to earn a little interest.

Summary

David had earned $1,100 by using his credit card to pay for his business expenses.

1. Sign-up bonus from credit card: $150
2. Five percent cash-back bonus from credit card: $75
3. Opening a checking account: $100
4. Opening a savings account: $100
5. Interest from $5,000: $25

6. Retention bonus from credit card: $50
7. One percent cash-back bonus from credit card: $600

A couple of months later, David gets a new idea about how to make more money from credit cards. You'll see David again in chapter 12, but first meet Tom and Diane.

CHAPTER 9

Tom Pays Off His Student Loan

In this chapter, you'll learn how to transfer a credit card balance without paying a balance-transfer fee.

Tom is an engaged twenty-five-year-old who graduated from college a couple of years ago. Like a lot of young college graduates, Tom had to take out a student loan to complete his collegiate work.

The student loan was a little over $18,000. He is paying down the loan every month with a $500 monthly payment. Since graduation, the loan has been reduced to around $8,000.

Tom hates paying the $500 a month, but he knows that without the loan he would not have his great job now. What irks Tom more than the loan is the interest he pays each and every month. He wishes he could have the entire $500 go to the principal and not pay any interest. Interest makes somebody else rich, not Tom.

He is engaged to a beautiful woman, and he wants to set a date for the nuptials. He wants to be debt free, but the student loan and its interest are keeping him in the red. Tom does not think it would be fair to his beloved to bring debt into the marriage. Figuring out how to solve this problem in a timely manner bothers Tom.

One of Tom's professors would tell Tom, "Use that thing between your skull bones. You need to be creative. You need to be imaginative. Do not think inside the box. Mediocrity is an excuse for a lack of imagination."

The company that offered Tom the credit card he carries around in his wallet recently sent Tom an offer of 0 percent financing for six months on all purchases. Tom does not use his credit card; he just keeps it in his wallet for emergencies.

The credit card company recently raised his credit limit to $12,000, which is more than enough to cover his student balance of around $8,000.

The credit card company has sent Tom some blank checks to draw on his credit card account. He would simply have to write a check to the student loan company from the credit card company— but there is a catch. The credit card company will charge Tom 5 percent for using the checks. The check acts like a balance transfer incurring a balance-transfer fee.

Tom will have nothing to do with this 5 percent balance-transfer fee. He uses the gray matter in his skull to solve the dilemma.

Tom's total monthly expenses are about $4,000 plus his $500 student loan payment. Tom realizes that all he needs to do is charge all of his monthly expenses for two months to his credit card. He will take two months of expenses ($8,000) and pay off the student loan. Then he will pay down the credit card with his usual $500 a month. Tom decides to do it!

In August, Tom pays all of his expenses with his credit card. He takes the $4,000 he would normally have used to pay his bills and sends it in as a payment on the student loan. He takes the $500 he usually sends to the student loan company and makes a payment to his credit card company instead.

The following graphic illustrates what Tom is doing to eliminate his student loan.

Tom's credit card
$4,000 charged
−$500 payment
$3,500 August balance

Tom's student loan
$8,000 balance
−$4,000 payment
$4,000 August balance

Tom does the same thing the next month. He charges his usual monthly expenses to his credit card. ($4,000). He pays the student loan off with the $4,000 he would have spent on his monthly expenses. He no longer has a student loan. He makes his usual $500 monthly payment to the credit card company.

Tom's credit card
$3,500 balance
+$4,000 charged
−$500 payment
$7,000 September balance

Tom's student loan
$4,000 balance
−$4,000 payment
0 September balance

Now, for the next four to five months, Tom will not be paying any interest. This makes Tom happy. Every month his full $500 payment will go toward the principal only on his student loan. He continues to make his usual $500 monthly payment.

Tom's credit card
$7,000 balance
−$500 payment
$6,500 October balance

Tom's credit card
$6,500 balance
−$500 payment
$6,000 November balance

Tom receives several credit card offers with differing promotions and incentives. In November, Tom decides which credit card he will use next to pay down his student loan without paying any interest. This one credit card company offers 0 percent financing for twelve months. This is what Tom wants and needs to eliminate his debt.

He reads the entire offer again to make sure he understands the details of the agreement. There is no annual fee. He fills out the application completely and signs it. He sends it off in the mail.

About a week later, the new credit card arrives in the mail. Tom calls the company number and activates the credit card. He puts it to use immediately.

Tom charges about $4,000 in his monthly expenses to his new credit card. He takes the $4,000 he would have used to pay his bills, and sends in a $4,000 payment to the old credit card company. He makes his usual $500 payment to the new credit card company.

The following illustrates what Tom is doing to eliminate his student loan/old credit card.

Tom's old credit card
$6,000 balance
−$4,000 payment
$2,000 December balance

Tom's new credit card
$4,000 charged
−$500 payment
$3,500 December balance

The next month, Tom watches how he charges. He only charges $2,000 of his monthly expenses to his new credit card. He takes the $2,000 he would have used to pay his bills, and he sends in a $2,000 payment to his old credit card company. He makes his usual $500 monthly payment to his new credit card.

Below is an illustration of what Tom does.

Tom's old credit card
$2,000 balance
−$2,000 payment
0 January balance

Tom's new credit card
$3,500 balance
$2,000 charged
−$500 payment
$5,000 January balance

Tom's old credit card is paid off. He will have his new credit card paid off in ten months at 0 percent financing. He will make a $500 payment for ten months.

1. February balance $4,500
2. March balance $4,000
3. April balance $3,500
4. May balance $3,000
5. June balance $2,500
6. July balance $2,000
7. August balance $1,500
8. September balance $1,000
9. October balance $ 500
10. November balance $ 0

It is done. Tom's student loan is paid off.

On December twenty-fourth, Tom marries the girl of his dreams on a beautiful Christmas Eve. As they leave the church, winter blesses the couple with the first snowfall of the season.

Summary

Tom did earn an extra $250 along the way in our story. His old credit card always offered a 1 percent cash-back bonus. He had charged $8,000 to transfer his student loan balance to his old credit card, which earned him $80 in cash-back bonus money.

His old credit card company allowed him to purchase gift cards. His new wife had a favorite department store where she liked to shop. His credit card company offered a $25 gift card for the price of twenty dollars. He received four twenty-five-dollar gift cards to his wife's favorite department store and gave them to her to spend as she wished.

The new credit card that Tom used to pay off the old credit card in $6,000 in purchases earned Tom a cash-back bonus of $150. He earned a hundred-dollar sign-up bonus after his first $1,000 in purchases. He earned sixty dollars off the $6,000 in purchases due to the 1 percent cash-back bonus offered.

The bonus could only be taken in increments of fifty dollars. This credit card company did not offer gift cards. He requested a $150 deposit into his checking account. It took about seventy-two hours for the deposit to be credited to his checking account.

Tom then called up the new credit card company and cancelled his account. Then he cut up his credit card. He still keeps his old credit card in his wallet to use in an emergency.

Some people would have used a balance transfer from Tom's old credit card to the new credit card for the $5,000 balance. That would have been great as long as the new credit card company would not have charged a balance transfer fee. Until recently, many credit card companies would not charge customers a balance transfer fee. But that is not the case today.

There is usually a 3 to 5 percent balance transfer fee when you transfer a balance from one credit card to another credit card. It is more common to see a 4 or 5 percent balance transfer fee. In the story, this would have cost Tom anywhere from $150 to $250 to do a balance transfer fee.

Tom is wiser. He does not want to pay for something he does not need or is a waste of money. Paying a balance transfer fee is a waste of hard-earned money and time.

This is how you avoid the balance transfer fee.

Let's say you have a $5,000 credit card balance (the same amount Tom had at one point in our story), but your credit card company is charging you interest at a rate of 18 percent. That is bad.

A credit card offer comes in the mail or online. They offer you eighteen months of 0 percent financing. The catch is that they want to charge you a 3 to 5 percent balance transfer fee. Which means they want to charge you anywhere from $150 to $250. They charge you this amount to send a check to the credit card company you currently have a balance with. Does this not seem ludicrous? You must bypass this outrageous fee.

Instead of transferring the $5,000 balance from the old credit card to the new credit card, you charge your monthly expenses to your new credit card. The money you would normally use for your monthly expenses you instead put toward the balance of the old credit card. This eventually brings the old credit card to a zero balance. Your old balance is transferred to the new credit card without a balance transfer fee.

For example, your monthly expenses are about $2,500. Charge all those expenses to your new credit card. Take the $2,500 you were going to use to pay your monthly expenses anyway and pay the old credit card with $2,500.

You will now have two credit card balances.

The old credit card has a $2,500 balance with an 18 percent annual interest rate.

The new credit card has a $2,500 balance with no interest charges.

Do the same thing the next month.

Your old credit card will have a zero balance.

The new credit card will have a $5,000 balance with no interest being charged. You have decided to make a $200 monthly payment until the debt is erased.

1. January balance $4,800 ($5,000-$200 payment)
2. February balance $4,600
3. March balance $4,400
4. April balance $4,200
5. May balance $4,000
6. June balance $3,800
7. July balance $3,600
8. August balance $3,400
9. September balance $3,200
10. October balance $3,000
11. November balance $2,800
12. December balance $2,600
13. January balance $2,400
14. February balance $2,200
15. March balance $2,000
16. April balance $1,800

In April, it is time to apply for a new credit card with 0 percent financing. The old credit card came with eighteen months of 0 percent financing. The eighteen months is up in June. Start the process of applying for a new credit card with 0 percent financing one to two months before the old credit card starts charging interest.

The new credit card arrives in May. You charge $1,800 in monthly expenses. The $1,800 you would have used to pay your monthly expenses goes toward the old credit card.

17. May payment of $1,800; balance on old credit card is $0.

You have decided to continue to make a $200 monthly payment until the debt is erased.

1. May balance $1,600 ($1,800-$200 payment)
2. June balance $1,400
3. July balance $1,200
4. August balance $1,000
5. September balance $800
6. October balance $600
7. November balance $400
8. December balance $200
9. January balance $ 0

That is how to avoid balance transfer fees and interest charges.

CHAPTER 10

Diane Pays for Braces

In this chapter, you'll learn how to pay off a credit card balance using sign-up bonuses and cash-back bonuses, and how to transfer a balance without incurring a balance transfer fee.

Diane is a single mother. Her twelve-year-old son needs braces. The orthodontist tells Diane that they can wait for about another three to four months. This will give Diane some time to come up with the money to pay for the braces.

Diane's dental insurance does not cover braces. She must pay for the braces out of pocket. The braces will cost $3,400.

The receptionist at the orthodontist's office says she can give Diane a 5 percent cash discount. She does not have the money.

The receptionist gives Diane the option of financing. Diane would pay $500 up front and finance the other $2,900 at 12 percent interest. She would pay $100 a month until the debt was paid. This is unacceptable to Diane. She does not pay interest. That is a waste of time and energy.

Even though she does not have the money right now, she tells the receptionist that she will pay cash and take the cash discount.

"Okay," says the receptionist, "That will be $3,400 minus the 5 percent cash discount which comes to $3,230. We'll round it down to $3,200."

Diane replies, "Well, the dentist says we can wait for three to four months. I have reservations about paying the entire bill up front today. When I was a child, my mother paid for my braces all up front; she paid for services that were not completely rendered. The orthodontist I was seeing had his office burn down. Instead of rebuilding and continuing his practice, the orthodontist retired. We had to find another orthodontist to complete the process. And we had to pay that orthodontist also. I would like to start the braces process in three months. I want to pay half of the bill then. I will pay the other half in six months."

She does not tell the receptionist that she is worried about her orthodontist completing the job because the orthodontist is two months pregnant. She is worried about history repeating itself.

The receptionist goes to the back office and talks over the deal with the office manager. Diane's terms are agreed to. Diane makes the appointment for her son in three months.

Now it is time to pay for the braces.

She already holds the credit card offer she would like to use. She reads the entire offer.

There is no annual fee.

There is a $100 sign-up bonus after $1,000 in purchases.

It comes with eighteen months of 0 percent financing and a 1 percent cash-back bonus on all purchases.

The cash-back bonus must be taken in increments of twenty-five dollars.

The credit card also comes with 5 percent cash back on gasoline and grocery purchases for six months.

When cashing in $300 or more in cash-back bonuses, you will receive an additional 25 percent bonus.

She fills out and signs the application, and then mails it in.

The credit card comes in the mail a couple of weeks later. When Diane calls to activate the credit card, the credit card company tries to sell Diane some credit protection services. She wisely declines to participate in the program.

Diane can charge about $2,600 a month on her credit card to pay some of her monthly bills.

Chargeable monthly bills

5 percent cash back*		1 percent cash back	
Gasoline	$400	Rent	$1,000
Groceries	$600	Cable	$150
	$1,000	Phone	$150
*(first 6 months)		Utilities	$ 300
			$1,600

In January, instead of paying the above expenses with her debit card, Diane charges all of the above expenses to her credit card. She goes to the credit card company's website and sets up her username and password. She pays the credit card company $1,000. She keeps the $1,600 and puts the money into her savings account. She does not have to surrender the first payment to the orthodontist until March.

In this month, Diane earns $166 in her cash-back bonus account. Diane qualifies for the hundred-dollar sign-up bonus because she has charged more than $1,000. She also earns fifty dollars off the $1,000 in purchases of gasoline and groceries, and she earns sixteen dollars from the other $1,600 she charged to her credit card. She does not use the bonus right away. This credit card comes with an additional 25 percent bonus when she cashes in $300 or more from her cash-back bonus account.

Month	Cash Back Earned	Cash Back Balance	Credit Card Balance
January	$166	$166	$1,600

For Diane, money is tight. She did not receive a raise this January. Nobody at her office did. To pay for the braces (or in other words to pay the credit card balance off), she adjusts her 401k contributions and her W-4 form at work. Every other week on payday she will go online and pay the credit card company fifty dollars.

In February, Diane again charges her monthly expenses to credit card ($2,600). She pays the credit card company $2,700. She would have used $2,600 to pay her bills; the additional one hundred dollars comes from the adjustments in her paycheck to pay down the credit card balance. She also earns sixty-six dollars in her cash-back bonus account due to her $2,600 in purchases.

Month	Cash Back Earned	Cash Back Balance	Credit Card Balance
Feb.	$66	$232	$1,500

At the beginning of March, Diane withdraws the $1,600 from her savings account and drags a reluctant twelve-year-old boy to the orthodontist's office. She pays the receptionist the $1,600, and the braces process for her son begins. He is not happy, but Diane is.

For the next four months, Diane continues to charge $2,600 to her credit card. Each month, she pays the credit card $2,700. She is continuing to rack up cash-back bonuses and bring down the balance on her credit card.

Month	Cash Back Earned	Cash Back Balance	Credit Card Balance
March	$66	$298	$1,400
April	$66	$364	$1,300
May	$66	$430	$1,200
June	$66	$496	$1,100

Unfortunately in June, The 5 percent cash-back bonus on gasoline and groceries expires. She is only going to earn 1 percent on the entire $2,600 charged to her credit card. This is a total twenty-six dollars cash back earned a month instead of sixty-six dollars—a difference of forty dollars a month.

Diane receives another offer from a credit card company offering a $150 sign-up bonus after the first purchase. The other details of the offer are not that important to Diane. She is sticking with the old credit card for next the next twelve months. She is just going to use this new credit card to make a quick buck and get out.

Diane gets the new credit card in June. She immediately activates the credit card. She charges $6.50 for two gallons of milk. She waits three days for the charges to post. She pays off the card right away.

In July, she requests her $150 sign-up bonus from the new credit card company. The $150 is deposited into Diane's checking account in about seventy-two hours. She then calls up the new credit card company and cancels the credit card account. Then she cuts up the credit card.

Diane makes a $150 payment to her credit card. The $150 sign-up bonus goes directly to paying for the braces.

The other $1,600 is now due at the orthodontist's office. This month, Diane continues to use her old credit card to pay her monthly expenses ($2,600). This month, Diane only makes a payment of $1,100. (The extra one hundred dollars is from her paycheck.) She takes the other $1,600 down to the orthodontist's office. She settles the account with the orthodontist. Now she only owes the credit card company money. Her new balance is $2,450.

Forwarded balance = $1,100 - $150 sign-up bonus - $100 monthly payment + $1,600 final braces payment = $2,450

The $2,450 appears disheartening to Diane. She's been making payments for six months, and the balance on her account is going up.

She ponders the situation for a while, and then she realizes that she is making progress. The beginning balance on the braces was $3,200; the balance is now $2,450. The balance has been reduced by $750, or nearly one quarter of the starting price. This makes Diane a little happier about the situation.

She is also pleased about the $150 sign-up bonus she took advantage of with the other credit card, and she sees a $496 cash-back bonus balance on her online credit card statement. She smiles to herself. She knows she is on the right track.

For the next ten months, Diane continues to charge her $2,600 in monthly expenses to her credit card. Each month she makes a $2,700 payment to the credit card company. She continues to accumulate cash-back bonuses.

Month	Cash Back Earned	Cash Back Balance	Credit Card Balance
July	$26	$522	$2,450
Aug.	$26	$548	$2,350
Sept.	$26	$574	$2,250
Oct.	$26	$600	$2,150
Nov.	$26	$626	$2,050
Dec.	$26	$652	$1,950
Jan.	$26	$678	$1,850
Feb.	$26	$704	$1,750
March	$26	$730	$1,650
April	$26	$756	$1,550
May	$26	$782	$1,450

In May, Diane responds to another credit card solicitation. She reads the entire offer to understand what she is getting into.

There is no annual fee.

There is a one-hundred-dollar sign-up bonus after $1,000 in purchases.

It comes with 0 percent financing.

There is a 1 percent cash-back bonus on all purchases. The cash-back bonus must be taken in increments of fifty dollars.

Diane fills out the application completely, signs it, and mails the application to the credit card company.

She receives her new credit card in the mail about ten days later and calls to activate it. She declines all the protection services the company offers to her.

It is time for Diane to request her cash-back bonus. She has earned $782. Unfortunately the terms of the agreement state that the cash-back bonus is to be taken in increments of twenty-five dollars; she misses out on seven dollars.

Diane requests that $775 be credited to her checking account. She will receive more than the $775 because she is cashing over $300 in cash-back bonuses. She receives an additional 25 percent bonus on her cash-back bonus, but this bonus is only applied to $675. The other one hundred is a sign-up bonus. The sign-up bonus is usually not included in the calculation of the additional 25 percent bonus.

She earns an additional $168.75. ($675 @ 25 percent equals $168.75) She earns a total of $943.75.

The $943.75 shows up in Diane's checking account in about seventy-two hours. She kicks in the additional $6.25 and makes an additional payment ($950) to the credit card company.

She now has a $500 balance. She is excited about getting this thing paid for and behind her.

She is going to use her new credit card to eliminate her debt completely.

In June, Diane uses her new credit card. She charges her usual $2,600 in monthly expenses on the new card. She sends in a $500 payment to the old credit card. The old credit card's balance is erased.

Diane calls the old credit card company that she has been using the last eighteen months and cancels her account. She cuts up the credit card.

Diane also makes a $2,200 payment to the new credit card company. The balance on the new credit card is now $400. She also earns a hundred-dollar sign-up bonus because she has charged over a $1,000 on her credit card. And, she earns twenty-six dollars for the 1 percent cash-back bonus. She now has $126 in her new cash-back account.

Month	Cash Back Earned	Cash Back Balance	Credit Card Balance
June	$126	$126	$400

In July, Diane continues to use her new credit card to charge all of her monthly expenses, which total $2,600. She makes her usual $2,700 payment to the credit card company. She earns an additional twenty-six dollars from the 1 percent cash back.

Month	Cash Back Earned	Cash Back Balance	Credit Card Balance
July	$26	$152	$300

August comes, and Diane is getting excited. The end is almost near. She charges $2,600 to her credit card. She makes a $2,700 payment to the credit card company. She again earns twenty-six dollars in her cash-back account.

Month	Cash Back Earned	Cash Back Balance	Credit Card Balance
August	$26	$178	$200

September is the last month that Diane is in debt.

She charges the $2,600 in monthly expenses to her credit card. This month she only makes a payment of $2,600, not the usual $2,700. She is going to use the cash-back bonus to pay off the remaining balance.

Month	Cash Back Earned	Cash Back Balance	Credit Card Balance
Sept.	$26	$204	$200

Diane goes online to the credit card company's website. She requests that $200 from her cash-back bonus be credited to her credit card balance.

The $200 credit card balance disappears about seventy-two hours later. The braces are now paid for. She gives a big sigh of relief.

Diane is very happy—but not as happy as her twelve year old son. In two weeks, he gets his braces off!

Summary

Through her intellect, Diane saved $1,493.75.

The original cost of the braces was $3,400.

Because she paid cash instead of financing, the cost of the braces was reduced by $200.

The next savings came from the credit card Diane used once and then canceled. This credit card company contributed $150 to the braces.

The big bonus came from the first credit card, which Diane used for eighteen months. This amounted to $943.75.

The last credit card added a $200 savings to the cost of the braces.

Starting Cost	$3,400
Cash Discount	−$200
Sign-up Bonus	−$150
First Credit Card	−$943.75
Last Credit Card	−$200
Total Cost	$1,906.25

Diane only paid $1,906.25 for something that cost $3,400. Wasn't she shrewd?

Chapter 11

David Buys a Certificate of Deposit

Back in chapter eight, David earned $1,100 by using his credit card for his personal business expenses.

David wants to make more money by paying his expenses with his credit card. He wishes to get compensated for paying his monthly expenses and household bills.

He is going to use the credit card company's money to buy certificate of deposits. He will buy a $10,000 certificate of deposit for a term of one year. Interest rates are currently very low. The best David is hoping for is 1.25 percent.

David's personal monthly expenses equal $4,000. He will be able to charge these bills to his credit card every month. He will also be able to charge $6,000 in business expenses from the small company he owns and operates. His total credit card charges will be $10,000 a month.

In December, David receives a new credit card, which he applied for in November.

This credit card comes with a one-hundred-dollar sign-up bonus after $500 in purchases.

It comes with a 1 percent cash-back bonus.

Every three months, the credit card comes with 5 percent cashback bonus on certain items. There is a $1,500 limit to the 5 percent cash-back award. David will take full advantage of these 5 percent cash-back awards every three months.

The card offers 0 percent financing for twelve months. David will take full advantage of this feature.

An additional 25 percent bonus is available if David redeems more than $300 at one time from his cash-back bonus account.

Gift cards are also offered in lieu of cash with their added extra bonus. This does not matter to David, though; he is focused on making money by paying his bills.

The credit card company provides David with a $20,000 credit limit on his credit card. This is more than enough for David. But David holds on to the belief that it is always good to have more than enough for that just-in-case scenario.

In January, David charges the $10,000 in household and business expenses to his credit card. He has the $10,000 to pay off the credit card, but he does not use the $10,000 to pay off the debt.

He goes to his local bank. He sits down with the banker he usually does business with. They barter over the rate of the certificate of deposit. David gets the banker to a rate of 1.25 percent on a $10,000 certificate of deposit for a term of twelve months.

For the January payment, David transfers into his checking account the $1,100 he earned over the last year by using his credit card.

He goes to the credit card company's website. He sets up the username and password. He pays the credit card company the $1,100. He will now carry an $8,900 balance on the credit card. This will be interest free due to 0 percent financing for twelve months.

His January bonus adds up to $260; it is calculated as follows:

David earned a hundred-dollar bonus for his first $500 in purchases. This will be the only time David receives this bonus from this credit card.

Every three months the credit card company offers a 5 percent cash-back bonus on certain things such as gasoline; hotel bills; groceries; drug store, department store, and home improvement store purchases; and more. There is a $1,500 limit on the 5 percent cash back. David spends the $1,500 on the promotional items offered this quarter. David earns seventy-five dollars from the 5 percent cash-back bonus.

David earns an additional eighty-five dollars from the 1 percent cash back earned on the $8,500 charged to the credit card. Again, David earns a total of $260 as a cash-back bonus. He will not cash in the cash-back bonus until the twelve months of 0 percent financing is over. David wants to earn the additional 25 percent bonus offered to David if he cashes in a cash-back bonus of over $300.

In February, David charges the $10,000 in household and business expenses to his credit card. He goes online, and he transfers $10,000 from his checking account to his credit card. This is his monthly payment for February. This month, David earns one hundred dollars as a cash-back bonus ($10,000 @ 1 percent). So far David's cash-back account is up to $360.

For the next nine months, David will charge $10,000 a month in expenses to his credit card. He will also make a $10,000 payment to his credit card company. Each month, David will carry the $8,900 balance interest free.

Month	Bonus Earned This Month	Total Cash Back Amount
March	$100	$460
April	$160	$620
May	$100	$720
June	$100	$820
July	$160	$980
August	$100	$1,080
September	$100	$1,180
October	$160	$1,340
November	$100	$1,440

Around the beginning of October, David started paying attention to all of the credit card offers coming in the mail and on the Internet. A couple of weeks later, David decides on a credit card.

This credit card offers 0 percent financing for eighteen months. There is a sign-up bonus of $150 after $1,000 in purchases. There is no annual fee. This card also comes with a 1 percent cash-back bonus on all purchases. This credit card also offers periodic (every three months) 5 percent cash-back bonuses with a purchase limit of $400.

David reads the entire offer to make sure he understands what he is signing up for. He fills out the entire application, signs it, and mails it.

About two weeks later he receives the new credit card. When he calls to activate the credit card, the credit card company representative tries to persuade David to take the credit protection services that the company offers. David kindly refuses. These services are a waste of money to the consumer, and David knows it.

David starts using his new credit card in December. He charges the usual $10,000 to his new credit card.

The old credit card has been carrying a balance of $8,900. David will now pay off the $8,900. There will be no more balances on this credit card.

David also makes a $1,100 payment to his new credit card. This will be his December monthly payment. David now has a $8,900 balance with the new credit card company.

David earns a cash-back bonus of $250 on his new credit card for the month of December. He earned $150 for making $1,000 in purchases, and he earned one hundred dollars as 1 percent cash back on the $10,000 in purchases.

In January, David's old credit card shows a cash-back bonus of $1,440. According to the credit card agreement, the cash-back bonuses must be taken in increments of fifty dollars.

To get to $1,450, David charges $1,000 on his monthly expenses to his old credit card. The he immediately pays off the credit card.

David charges the other $9,000 in January's monthly expenses to his new credit card. He makes a $9,000 payment to his new credit card.

In January, David earns an additional $106 from his $9,000 in purchases. He takes advantage of the 5 percent cash-back bonus on the $400 in the periodic promotion offered by the credit card company. He earns the usual 1 percent on the $8,600. His cash-back balance is $356.

Also in January, David renews his $10,000 certificate of deposit at the bank. David earns $125 in interest over the year.

In February, David makes his usual $10,000 in charges to his new credit card. He makes a $10,000 payment to his new credit card. He earns one hundred dollars as a cash-back bonus this month. The cash-back balance on the new credit card is now $456.

In February, David's cash-back bonus is up to date on the first credit card. The balance of his cash-back bonus account is $1,450. He requests that the entire balance be deposited to his checking account. David will also receive an additional $337.50. The $337.50 is a 25 percent bonus earned on cashing in more than $300 in cash-back bonuses. David earns a total of $1,787.50.

In February, David makes an additional payment to the new credit card company. He makes a payment of $1,900 ($1,787.50 and the $125, rounded down to $1,900). David's new outstanding balance on his credit card is $7,000 ($8,900-$1,900=$7,000).

David now calls the old credit card company and cancels his credit card account. He cuts up the credit card. He will now only use the new credit card for the next fourteen months.

For the next fourteen months, David continues to make his $10,000 in charges every month on his credit card. He also makes a $10,000 payment to his credit card every month. Each month, David carries forward a $7,000 balance at 0 percent financing.

Month	Bonus Earned This Month	Total Cash Back Amount
March	$100	$556
April	$116	$672
May	$100	$772
June	$100	$872
July	$116	$988
August	$100	$1,088

September	$100	$1,188
October	$116	$1,304
November	$100	$1,404
December	$100	$1,504
January	$116	$1,620
February	$100	$1,720
March	$100	$1,820
April	$116	$1,936

In January, David's certificate of deposit becomes due. He renews his $10,000 certificate of deposit for only six months this time. He has earned $125 over the last year off of his certificate of deposit. He puts the $125 in his savings account.

At the end of March, David finds a new credit card to use. This one offers a hundred-dollar sign-up bonus after $500 in purchases. It comes with 1 percent cash-back bonus. There are no periodic 5 percent cash-back bonuses. There is no annual fee. It comes with 0 percent financing for twelve months.

In May, David charges his usual $10,000 in monthly expenses to his new credit card.

David makes a $7,000 payment to his old credit card. The balance is now zero.

David makes a $3,000 payment to his new credit card. David now has the $7,000 balance on his new credit card.

David now has $200 in his cash-back bonus account on his new credit card. He earns a one-hundred-dollar sign-up bonus after the first $500 in purchases. He earns one hundred dollars from the 1 percent cash back on the $10,000 in purchases.

In May, David requests his cash-back bonus from his old credit card. The amount in the cash-back bonus account is $1,936. He can only request $1,925 (the cash-back bonus can only be taken increments of $25). The $1,925 is credited to his checking account about three days later.

He calls the old credit card company and cancels the account. He cuts up the credit card. He will now only use the new credit card.

David earns $2,050 ($125 in January from the certificate of deposit, and $1,925 from the cash-back bonus from the credit card company). David makes a $2,000 payment to the credit card company. The new credit card balance is $5,000.

In June, David charges $10,000 to his credit card for his monthly expenses. He makes a $10,000 payment to his credit card. He earns one hundred dollars in his cash-back bonus account. His cash-back bonus balance is now $300.

In July, David's six-month $10,000 certificate of deposit matures. He earns seventy-five dollars in interest.

David takes $5,000 to send in as a payment to the credit card company. This will eliminate the credit card balance completely.

David opens a new certificate of deposit in the amount of $5,125 for six months. The extra $125 comes from the seventy-five dollars in interest that he earned on the six-month certificate of deposit and the extra fifty dollars he earned from the old credit card.

David no longer carries a balance on his credit cards. He uses the cash-back bonuses to increase the amount of his certificate of deposits.

Month	Bonus Earned This Month	Total Cash Back Amount
July	$100	$400
August	$100	$500
September	$100	$600
October	$100	$700
November	$100	$800
December	$100	$900
January	$100	$1,000

In December, David requests $800 from his cash-back bonus account. He wants to add the $800 to his certificate of deposit, which comes due in January.

In January, the certificate of deposit matures. David earns thirty-two dollars in interest. David adds the thirty-two dollars in interest and the $800 from the cash-back bonus to the certificate of deposit. David opens a $5,957 certificate of deposit for a term of one year.

Each month for the following year, David charges $10,000 in monthly expenses to his credit card. Each month he pays the credit card balance in full. He never carries a balance.

Month	Bonus Earned This Month	Total Cash Back Amount
February	$100	$300
March	$100	$400
April	$100	$500
May	$100	$600
June	$100	$700
July	$100	$800
August	$100	$900
September	$100	$1,000
October	$100	$1,100
November	$100	$1,200
December	$100	$1,300
January	$100	$1,400

In December, David requests $1,200 from his cash-back bonus account. He wants to add the $1,200 to his certificate of deposit, which comes due in January.

In January, David earns seventy-five dollars in interest from the matured certificate of deposit. David adds the seventy-five dollars and the $1,200 cash-back bonus to his certificate of deposit.

He opens a $7,232 certificate of deposit for a term of one year.

David continues to pay his bills year after year with a credit card that pays him to pay his bills. He rolls over the interest and the cash-back bonuses into his certificate of deposit.

Summary

In four years, David earned $7,232 off the credit card company's money!

Instead of paying his bills with his checking account and his debit card, he used his credit card. He then either carried a balance with 0 percent financing, or he paid off the credit card balance entirely.

He never paid an annual fee.

He never paid a transfer fee.

He never paid any interest.

The credit card company made money off the merchants.

David made money off the credit card company.

Both parties in this agreement made money.

Both parties made money by moving money around. That is easy money.

CHAPTER 12

Mary and John Pay Off Their Truck

In this chapter, you'll learn how to avoid paying interest and fees using credit cards.

Mary and John are a couple in their early thirties. Like quite a few young marrieds, they were not very conscientious about their credit scores. Paying bills before there due date was not a priority for John when he was in his twenties. Mary moved quite a bit when she was younger. Mary did not always leave a forwarding address, so she missed some payments.

They, like most people, became more aware of the importance of paying their bills on time as they grew older and wiser.

Mary and John bought a new truck about four years ago. With a sizable down payment, they were able to qualify for a six-year loan at an interest rate of 13 percent. The original balance of the loan was $15,000. Four years later, they still owe around $5,200. They have a monthly payment of $301 a month.

Mary is the one who handles the bills in the family. A few years into their marriage, both Mary and John realized that only one person should handle paying the bills, and Mary became responsible for making all the payments on time.

Mary grew in wisdom during this time about how much her family was paying in interest on various loans. It made her sick to her stomach.

She reads books on personal finances. She listens to radio personalities about personal finances. One common theme among the financial gurus that is repeated often is that the best way to get out of debt is to pay off the lowest debt first. For Mary and John this is their truck.

They still have twenty-four monthly payments of $301 on the truck. The loan balance is $5,200, but a quick mathematical calculation on her computer's desktop calculator shows that their payments will amount to $7,224 (24 × $301 = $7,224). Mary is dumbfounded; she and John are obligated to pay $2,024 in interest over the next two years.

Mary received a credit card offer in the mail from one of the leading banks. Its tempting offer is a fifty-dollar bonus for making $1,000 in purchases. She reasons to herself that it would be easy to make $1,000 in their everyday purchases. She would just pay off the card with the money she is going to spend on the items anyway, and she will incur no interest charges by paying off the balance right away. Her plan all depends upon her acceptance from the credit card company.

Two weeks later, Mary receives her new credit card. It comes with a fifty-dollar sign-up bonus after $1,000 in purchases. Also with every purchase she earns 1 percent cash back. This 1 percent cash-back bonus can be withdrawn in increments of fifty dollars. So, Mary would have to make $5,000 in purchases to earn an additional fifty dollars.

The option of 0 percent financing for nine months catches Mary's attention. An idea is born in Mary's mind.

She pays most of the bills online with her debit card. All of her bill companies accept credit card payments without charging any service fees except her mortgage company, power company, and auto loan company. Why not pay all the bills with her credit card and earn 1 percent cash back?

The wheels of the human imagination continue to churn.

"We have about $2,600 in expenses a month. This includes monthly bills, groceries, gasoline, and incidentals. Two months of these expenses equal the $5,200 we owe on the truck. I could charge our expenses for two months and use the $5,200 to pay off the truck. I would only have to pay the credit card $217 a month to pay off the truck/credit card in twenty-four months. This would reduce my truck payment from $301 to $217 a month. This would be a savings of eighty-four dollars a month with no interest being charged to the debt."

Mary tells John her plan. He is not thrilled about it. He says they'll only get into trouble by playing around with credit cards. "What happens in nine months when the interest rate kicks in? What will we do then?" John asks.

Mary continues, "In about seven months you or I will accept another no-interest card credit card offer that we will receive in the mail. We can transfer the balance to the new credit card for their introductory 0 percent financing period."

"And then pay a balance-transfer fee? Doesn't that defeat the whole purpose of an interest-free card? They charge anywhere from 3 to 5 percent of the amount transferred." John is getting frustrated.

Mary remains calm. "We do not have to do a balance transfer."

John interrupts, "But you just said we would transfer the balance to the new interest-free card. That would induce a 3 to 5 percent balance-transfer fee."

"I would not use a balance transfer," Mary continues. "I would charge our monthly bills to the new credit card and pay off the old credit card with the money I would have used for the bills. This way I run up a tab on the new card and pay off the old card at the same time. No balance transfer fees will be charged. And, no interest will be charged."

"I'm going to leave this in your hands, Mary," says John, beginning to get the picture. "Sounds like you have it under control."

"Thank you John," replies Mary. "I won't let you down."

Mary pays all of her bills and expenses for January on her new credit card. She takes the $2,600 (which she would have paid her bills with), and sends in a $2,600 check for the truck loan.

Mary also pays $217 to her credit card. This would have been her truck payment.

The January balance on the truck loan is $2,600.

The credit card balance for January is $2,383 ($2,600-$217 payment =$2,383).

Mary again pays all of her expenses with her new credit card in February. She takes the $2,600 and pays off the truck loan.

Truck loan = $0 (yippee!)

Mary earns her fifty-dollar sign-up bonus (this bonus is for her first $1,000 in charges). This bonus shows up on her credit card statement. She goes online to the credit card company and cashes in her fifty-dollar bonus. Mary applies the fifty-dollar bonus directly to her credit card balance. While she is cashing in her fifty-dollar sign-up bonus, she makes her $217 monthly payment to the credit card company.

Credit card
> $2,383
> +2,600 (remaining truck balance)
> −$50 (bonus)
> −$217 (payment)
> =$4,716 February balance

Mary is thrilled about paying no interest. When she received the fifty-dollar bonus she was even more excited. She now realizes that she has made $5,200 in purchases. This will give her another fifty-dollar bonus due to the 1 percent cash back on all purchases.

Mary decides to continue to pay all of her monthly bills with this credit card and earn a cash-back bonus by paying her bills. She will charge about $2,600 in expenses a month (charges she would incur anyway), and she will pay the $2,600 to the credit card each month. Plus she will pay $217 a month toward her balance.

In March, Mary pays all of her expenses with her credit card. She charges $2,600.

Mary's new bonus of fifty dollars from $5,200 in purchases shows up on her statement. She cashes in her fifty-dollar bonus and applies it to her loan balance. She also makes a payment of $2,817 ($2,600 in monthly bills and her $217 payment).

Credit card

> $4,716
> +$2,600 (new charges)
> −$2,600 (pay for new charges)
> −$50 (bonus)
> <u>−$217 (payment)</u>
> $4,449 March balance

April comes, and Mary is comfortable and familiar with paying all of her expenses with her credit card. Her expenses again come to around $2,600 this month. She puts these expenses on her credit card. She makes a payment of $2,817 ($2,600 in monthly bills and her $217 payment).

Credit card

> $4,449
> +$2,600 (new charges)
> −$2,600 (pay for new charges)
> <u>−$217 (payment)</u>
> $4,232 April balance

In May, Mary earns another fifty-dollar bonus. This bonus is earned from her $5,200 in purchases in March and April. She again spends $2,600 on her monthly expenses and makes a payment of $2,817 ($2,600 in monthly bills and her $217 payment).

Credit card

$4,232
+$2,600 (new charges)
−$2,600 (pay for new charges)
−$50 (bonus)
−$217 (payment)
$3,965 May balance

In June, Mary responds to a new credit card offer she has received in the mail. This card offers a hundred-dollar sign-up bonus after $1,000 in purchases, 1 percent cash back, and 0 percent financing for sixteen months. The sixteen months would eliminate the truck balance completely. She hopes she qualifies.

She continues to pay all of her expenses with her credit card. The total again is around $2,600. She makes a payment of $2,817 ($2,600 in monthly bills and her $217 payment).

Credit card

$3,965
+$2,600 (new charges)
−$2,600 (pay for new charges)
−$217 (payment)
$3,748 June balance

In July, Mary earns another fifty-dollar bonus. This bonus is earned from $5,200 in purchases in May and June. She again spends $2,600 on her monthly expenses. She makes a payment of $2,817 ($2,600 in monthly bills and her $217 payment).

Credit card

$3,748
+$2,600 (new charges)
−$2,600 (pay for new charges)
−$50 (bonus)
−$217 (payment)
$3,481 July balance

Mary is accepted for the new credit card. She starts using it right away. She charges her new credit card the $2,600 for the month of August. Mary pays $2,817 ($2,600 + $217) to the old card.

Old Credit Card
> $3,481
> −$2,600 (payment for new charges)
> <u>−$217 (payment)</u>
> $664 August balance

The new credit card balance for August is $2,600.

In September, Mary uses her new credit card and charges $2,600 for expenses. She has received a one-hundred-dollar sign-up bonus on her new credit card statement. She goes online and cashes in her sign-up bonus, applying the bonus to her new credit card balance.

Mary pays off the $664 balance on first credit card; she acts like a balance transfer of $664 has occurred to her new credit card.

Old Credit Card
> $0

New Credit Card
> $2,600
> +$2,600 (from new charges)
> −$1,936 (pay for new charges*)
> −$100(bonus for first $1000 in purchases)
> <u>−$217(payment)</u>
> $2,947 September balance

* not the $2,600 because $2,600 − $664 (for paying off the old credit card) equals $1,936

In October, Mary charges $2,600 in expenses on her new credit card. She makes a payment of $2,817 ($2,600 in monthly bills and her $217 payment).

New Credit Card

$2,947
+$2,600 (from new charges)
−$2,600 (pay for new charges)
−$217 (payment)
$2,730 October balance

In November, a fifty-dollar bonus shows up on Mary's credit card statement. She cashes in her fifty-dollar bonus (from her September and October purchases) and applies it to her balance. She puts all her monthly expenses on her credit card ($2,600).

New Credit Card

$2,730
+$2,600 (new charges)
−$2,600 (pay for new charges)
−$50 (bonus)
−$217 (payment)
$2,463 November balance

December comes, and Mary remains faithful to the plan laid out. She charges $2,600 on her credit card. She makes a payment of $2,817 ($2,600 in monthly bills and her $217 payment).

New Credit Card

$2,436
+$2,600 (new charges)
−$2,600 (pay for new charges)
−$217(payment)
$2,246 December balance

Another fifty-dollar bonus shows up on Mary's January credit card statement. She has charged $5,200 in November and December to earn this bonus. She goes online and applies her fifty-dollar bonus to her outstanding balance. She charges $2,600 in monthly expenses to her credit card; then she makes a payment of $2,817 ($2,600 in monthly bills and her $217 payment).

New Credit Card
>$2,246
>+$2,600 (new charges)
>−$2,600 (pay for new charges)
>−$50 (bonus)
>−$217 (payment)
>$1,979 January balance

In February, Mary charges $2,600 on her credit card. She makes a payment of $2,817 ($2,600 in monthly bills and her $217 payment).

New Credit Card
>$1,979
>+$2,600 (new charges)
>−$2,600 (pay for new charges)
>−$217(payment)
>$1,762 February balance

A fifty-dollar bonus is given to Mary for $5,200 in purchases in the months of January and February. Mary applies her fifty-dollar bonus to her balance. She charges $2,600 to credit card in March. Then she makes a payment of $2,817 ($2,600 in monthly bills and her $217 payment).

New Credit Card
>$1,762
>+$2,600 (new charges)
>−$2,600 (pay for new charges)
>−$50 bonus
>−$217 (payment)
>$1,495 March balance

In April, Mary charges $2,600 in expenses to her credit card. Then she makes a payment of $2,817 ($2,600 in monthly bills and her $217 payment).

New Credit Card
$1,495
+$2,600 (new charges)
−$2,600 (pay for new charges)
−$217 (payment)
$1,278 April balance

May brings another fifty-dollar bonus to Mary's account. She had charged $5,200 in the months of March and April. She applies the fifty-dollar bonus to her balance. She charges $2,600 of monthly expenses to her credit card. Then she makes a payment of $2,817 ($2,600 in monthly bills and her $217 payment).

New Credit Card
$1,278
+$2,600 (new charges)
−$2,600 (pay for new charges)
−$50 (bonus)
−$217 (payment)
$1,011 May balance

Mary and John's balance is now around $1,000. They are getting excited about not having a $217 a month payment much longer. They have started planning a getaway to celebrate!

In June, Mary continues to charge $2,600 a month for their monthly expenses. Then she makes a payment of $2,817 ($2,600 in monthly bills and her $217 payment).

New Credit Card
$1,011
+$2,600 (new charges)
−$2,600 (pay for new charges)
−$217 (payment)
$794 June balance

In July, Mary cashes in another fifty-dollar bonus and applies it to her balance. She charges $2,600 on her credit card to pay her monthly expenses. Then she makes a payment of $2,817 ($2,600 in monthly bills and her $217 payment).

New Credit Card
$794
+$2,600 (new charges)
−$2,600 (pay for new charges)
−$50 (bonus)
−$217(payment)
$527 July balance

In August, Mary charges $2,600 on her credit card. She makes a payment of $2,817 ($2,600 in monthly bills and her $217 payment).

New Credit Card
$527
+$2,600 (new charges)
−$2,600 (pay for new charges)
−$217 (payment)
$310

This will be the last month in which Mary and John carry a balance on this credit card. Mary charges her usual expenses for the month ($2,600). This September she also earns another fifty-dollar bonus from her charges in July and August. She applies this bonus to her balance. She will also make her usual payment of $2,817 ($2,600 in monthly bills and her $217 payment) to her credit card account. She will also send in an additional amount of forty-three dollars to take the account down to a zero balance.

New Credit Card
$310
+$2,600 (new charges)
−$2,600 (pay for new charges)
−$50 (bonus)
−$217 (payment)
<u>−$43 (additional amount)</u>
$0

The truck is now paid off.

Summary

The truck was paid in twenty-one months with payments of $217 instead of twenty-four months of $301 payments. There was no interest paid on the truck loan during these last twenty-one months.

Besides paying no interest, Mary has earned eleven sign-up and cash-back bonuses during these twenty-one months.

1. February sign-up bonus after $1,000 in purchases: $50
2. March 1 percent cash back on $5,000 in charges: $50
3. May 1 percent cash back on $5,000 in charges (May): $50
4. July 1 percent cash back on $5,000 in charges: $50
5. September sign-up bonus after $1,000 in purchases on new credit card: $100
6. November 1 percent cash back on $5,000 in charges: $50
7. January 1 percent cash back on $5,000 in charges: $50
8. March 1 percent cash back on $5,000 in charges: $50

9. May 1 percent cash back on $5,000 in charges: $50
10. July 1 percent cash back on $5,000 in charges (July): $50
11. September 1 percent cash back on $5,000 in charges (September): $50

Mary has earned $600 by just paying her ordinary bills and expenses with her credit card. Mary has also saved $2,024 in interest by using her credit cards to help pay off the truck loan. Mary and John have saved $2,624. They saved this $2,624 by using their credit cards wisely and by just by paying their monthly expenses with their credit cards.

CHAPTER 13

Granny Pays for Christmas

Granny is a sweet little old lady. The kind of woman anyone would want for a grandmother.

Her biggest source of income is her monthly social security check. She lives from month to month.

Christmas is always a financial burden to Granny. She just does not have an extra $500 or $600 to spend on holiday gifts. She likes to spoil her grandchildren, but the cost of Christmas seems to go up every year.

Around the middle of September, Granny receives a credit card offer in the mail, which will take care of the Christmas dilemma this year.

This credit card offers $500 in gift cards to various stores after charging $500 on the credit card. The deal sounds too good to true. She starts reading the offer.

The credit card charges an annual fee. The annual fee is waived for the first year. That is perfect for Granny. She is only going to use the credit card to get the $500 in gift cards. Then she is going to cancel the credit card.

The rest of the offer seems legitimate. She reads it again to make sure she knows what she is signing up for. She does not want to be another senior who gets taken advantage of.

Granny fills out the application completely, signs it, and sends it off in the mail.

About two weeks later, Granny's shiny silver new credit card arrives in the mail. She calls to activate her credit card, and the representative from the credit card company tries to sell Granny on some credit protection services. Granny kindly declines the solicitations.

Granny's six-month car insurance premium is due; it costs Granny $700 every six months. She has the money to pay the bill now, but she is going to pay the bill this time with the credit card. Then she is going to pay off the credit card with the money. She will not carry a balance.

Granny goes online to the insurance company. Instead of paying her bill with her debit card, she chooses a new method of payment, her new credit card. It takes all of two minutes to make the change in payments.

A week later, Granny goes to the credit card company's website. She sets up her username and password. She pays the entire $700 balance. She looks over the online statement to see if her account has been credited with her bonus, but the bonus has not been credited to her account yet.

Granny checks the website again in two weeks for the posting of her bonus to her account. It is not in there.

She checks again two weeks later. The bonus part of her online statement is empty.

It is now the beginning of November. Christmas is coming fast. Granny decides to call the credit card company to see when the gift cards will be available.

The credit card company's representative assures Granny that she has qualified for the $500 in gift cards. The bonus will show up in her November statement, but she can send out the gift cards now if that is what Granny wants.

Granny asks for the gift cards now.

The gift cards come in fifty-dollar gift cards. The representative asks Granny which store she would like to have a gift card or gift cards to.

Granny chooses ten fifty-dollar gift cards to her favorite department store. The representative lets Granny know that she will receive the gift cards in about seven to ten days.

Granny receives the gift cards. There are no telephone numbers to call to activate. There are no restrictions.

She goes to the department store to do her Christmas shopping. The department store is currently offering a special promotion. For every fifty dollars in purchases, the shopper receives ten dollars in department store cash when the shopper uses the department store's credit card. The shopper cannot use the department store cash on the same day.

Granny wants to take advantage of the special promotion; she does carry the department store's credit card in her purse. She goes to the customer service department.

She asks the sales associate if she can use her department store credit card to pay for her purchases so she can take advantage of the store's special promotion, and then pay off the credit card with her gift cards. She is told that she cannot pay her department store credit card with the gift cards.

The sales associate does explain to Granny how to still receive the store's special promotion. She has to spend fifty dollars to receive ten dollars in the department store's cash. Granny only has to put one dollar on the store's credit card, and then she can use her gift cards to pay the rest of her balance. So, if Granny buys $500's worth of gifts, she can put one dollar on her credit card, and she can use the gift cards for the remaining $499. She would then receive one hundred dollars of department store cash.

Granny is thrilled.

She does all of her Christmas shopping at her favorite department store. Besides the special department store cash promotion, most of the store has some special sale going on. Granny is saving more money.

Granny goes to pay for her items. The bill comes to $512.34 (she watched the tally closely as she shopped). She first pays $12.34 on her department store's credit card. She pays the remaining $500 with her ten fifty-dollar gift cards.

The sales associate hands Granny ten certificates. Each certificate is worth ten dollars. This is the department store's cash promotion. The certificates are to be used during the first seven days of December.

After receiving the certificates, she asks the sales lady if she can pay her credit card bill right there and then. Yes, she can, and so she does pay the $12.34. She now has no balance on the department store's credit card.

Granny's Christmas shopping is done.

She calls the credit card company that gave her the $500 in gift cards. She tells the credit card representative that she would like to cancel her credit card.

The representative asks why she would like to cancel her credit card.

Granny kindly tells the representative that she only signed up for the credit card to receive the $500 in gift cards.

The representative states that the credit card company would hate to lose a valuable customer like Granny. They offer Granny fifty dollars to stay with them. She can take the fifty dollars in a gift card or apply it to a future balance. And, if Granny charges $1,000 on the credit card, they will credit her account with another fifty dollars.

Granny repeats the information back to the representative; this is to make sure she understands what she is hearing. She tells the representative to keep her as a customer. The representative tells Granny her account will be credited with the fifty dollars immediately.

The next day, Granny drives her old pick-up to the gas pump at the local convenience store. She pulls out the credit card she was going to cancel. She fills up the gas tank. As she is nearing the fifty-dollar mark she slows down. She only wants to put in fifty dollars. This is to take advantage of the fifty-dollar credit on her credit card. She misses the mark. The total comes to $50.01.

A couple of days later, she goes online to the credit card company's website. She pays the penny balance. She laughs to herself. "If only every bill was this low," she says to herself.

During the first week in December, there is a big sale on silverware at Granny's department store. Over the years, Granny has lost spoons and forks here and there, so now she is going to replace her silverware. It is safe to say that it may have been over thirty years since Granny bought new silverware.

Also, a couple items she recently bought from the department store are now selling at a lower price. She is going to get the price difference.

Once at the department store, Granny goes to customer service department. The line is long this time of year, but she patiently waits her turn. She explains about the difference in prices, and she gives the sales associate her receipts. Granny gets back $22.45.

Granny then goes shopping for her silverware. She finds what she wants. The sales price is one hundred dollars.

She goes to the checkout line. She again has to wait a while due to the holiday shopping season. The total with tax comes to $108. She pays with the one hundred dollars in department store cash, and she makes up the difference with the department store's credit card. They are again offering the same promotion.

The sales associate at the checkout line gives Granny two more ten-dollar certificates. These must be used during the first week of January.

Granny then pays off the eight-dollar balance on the store's credit card. She tells the sales associate that she will see her in January.

With the extra $14.45 she treats herself to lunch at the fast food Chinese restaurant. Granny loves Chinese food.

Granny decides not to charge $1,000 on the credit card to receive the extra fifty dollars. She wants to keep her life simple.

Granny calls the credit card company to cancel the credit card. This time, Granny gets past the credit card representative's pleas. She cancels the credit card and then cuts the card up.

Summary

Granny had no financial worries this past Christmas. She literally made money out of thin air.

She earned $500 in gift cards for purchasing over $500 on her credit card.

She also earned an additional $120 in department store cash.

And, she earned fifty dollars for staying with the credit card a little longer.

She paid no interest.

She paid no annual fee.

Granny used the credit card twice. She received $670 for using the credit card. That was quite a deal!

In January, Granny took advantage of the twenty dollars in department store cash. This she used for an upcoming birthday present. She wished those credit card deals would come every month!

CHAPTER 14

A Unique Way to Fund an IRA

It is the end of January, and Scott is preparing his tax returns. He always receives a refund. That is why he starts doing his taxes earlier than most people. He wants his money back.

After the mortgage deduction, real estate deduction, charitable giving deduction, dependent deductions, child tax credits, and his measly traditional IRA contribution, Scott is set to receive a $3,600 refund from the IRS.

The $3,600 is a nice sum of money to get back, but Scott wonders about his lacking IRA. He is $3,000 short of the maximum contribution limit for the year.

He decides to use the upcoming refund money to reach the maximum contribution for the past year.

He can wait for the refund to be posted to his checking account. After he has received the funds from the IRS, he can still make a $3,000 contribution to his IRA for the previous year; the deadline last year's contribution is April 15.

Scott refuses that scenario. If he makes an IRA contribution after he files his tax return, Scott will have to file an amended return. This raises the probability of an audit. Scott wants to keep any contact with the IRS to a minimum.

Scott then has an "Aha!" moment. He is doing the taxes on his laptop, but at the same time he has his favorite social network website open on his laptop screen too. The site is advertising credit cards with 0 percent financing for various lengths of time.

Scott does not feel comfortable applying for a credit card online, but he knows there are a couple of credit card solicitations in the week-old pile of mail on the kitchen counter.

He saves his work on his taxes and logs off his computer.

He checks the accumulation of mail. There are two credit card offers in the mass of mail. They both offer 0 percent financing for twelve months, which is more than enough time for Scott.

But first, Scott pulls out the old trusty credit card he has used for years. He calls the telephone number on the back of the credit card. He goes through the menu of options, and he finally reaches a person he can talk to.

He asks the credit card representative for 0 percent financing for six months. (To Scott, it does not hurt to ask. It would be easier for him if his old credit card company would give him 0 percent financing for six months.)

The representative tells Scott no on the 0 percent financing, but she can offer 1.9 percent for six months.

Scott thanks her for the 1.9 percent financing and ends the conversation. At least he has a better rate on his credit card for six months, but he is not going to use it.

He reads over the offers from both credit card companies. They both offer the 0 percent financing for twelve months with no annual fee. He decides to go with the credit card offering the bigger sign-up bonus: $150 after $1,000 in purchases.

He fills out the application completely, signs it, and mails it.

About seven days later, his shimmering new credit card arrives in the mail. He calls the telephone number on the front of the card to activate his credit card. He declines all of the protection services the representative tries to sell him.

He pays all of his monthly expenses with his new credit card. He charges $4,000 on the card.

He has the money to pay off the credit card, but he will use the $4,000 to fund his IRA and make a monthly credit card payment. He takes $3,000 and fully funds his IRA for the previous year. He has contributed the full $5,000, and this makes Scott happy.

Scott corrects his tax return to reflect a $5,000 traditional IRA contribution. The extra $3,000 contribution increases his tax return by $450. His refund will now total $4,050.

Scott goes to the credit card company's website. He sets up his username and password. He uses the $1,000 to make a credit card payment. He owes the credit card company $3,000.

About three weeks later, his tax refund is deposited in his checking account ($4,050).

He wastes no time. He goes to the credit card company's website. He is about to pay the $3,000 balance when he notices the bonus section on his online statement.

The $150 sign-up bonus is already listed in the bonus section. He applies the $150 to the credit card balance and then makes a $2,850 payment. The balance is now zero on the credit card.

About a week later, Scott calls the credit card company, and he cancels the credit card account. He then cuts up the credit card.

Scott finds the process of using his tax refund to fully fund his IRA a good idea. He is going to have his tax refund pay for his IRA contribution.

This year with a $2,000 contribution, his tax refund would have been $3,600. Without the $2,000 contribution, his tax return would have been $3,300. (His top income level is taxed at the 15 percent rate.)

To increase his tax refund to $5,000 to fully fund his IRA, Scott will have to increase the amount of money his employer withholds from his paycheck.

He needs $1,700 more a year withheld from his check. He is paid every two weeks. He simply divides $1,700 by twenty-six pay periods. This amounts to withholding an additional $65.38 a paycheck. Scott will round up this amount to seventy dollars a paycheck to ensure he has enough money.

Scott adjusts his W-4 at work. On line 6 of the W-4 ("additional amount, if any, you want withheld from each paycheck"), he writes, "$70."

In December, Scott wastes no time. He finds another credit card company offering 0 percent financing. This credit card comes with a one-hundred-dollar sign-up bonus, and it does not have an annual fee.

The new credit card arrives near the end of December. He activates the card.

In January, Scott charges $4,000 in monthly expenses on his credit card.

He goes to the credit card company's website. He sets up his username and password. He makes a $1,500 payment to the credit card company. He retains $2,500 to put toward his IRA contribution.

In February, Scott charges $4,000 in monthly expenses to his credit card. He makes a $1,500 payment to his credit card company. Scott's current credit card balance is $5,000.

He takes February's $2,500 and January's $2,500, and he makes a $5,000 contribution to his traditional IRA. He has now fully funded his IRA for the previous year.

He immediately sets to work doing his taxes. This year's tax return shows a $5,000 traditional IRA contribution. Scott is happy.

Scott's tax refund this year is $5,100.

About three weeks later, the $5,100 is deposited into Scott's checking account.

He goes to the credit card company's website. He applies the hundred-dollar sign-up bonus he had earned to his credit card balance. He then makes a $4,900 payment. The credit card balance is now zero.

One week later, Scott cancels the credit card and cuts it up.

Every year, Scott will repeat the process to fully fund his traditional IRA.

Summary

Every year, Scott will repeat the process to fully fund his traditional IRA.

In December, Scott will apply for a new credit card offering 0 percent financing for a certain period of time. He will also choose a credit card that comes with a sign-up bonus.

He will charge January and February's monthly expenses to his credit card. He will accumulate enough cash from those two months to fund his IRA for the last year.

His IRS refund will cover the credit card charges. He will pay off the credit card with the IRS refund.

He will then cancel and cut up his credit card. Every year, his IRA will be fully funded.

CHAPTER 15

Buy a Used Car with a Credit Card

Sherri's car is old. The tires are bald. Every time she steps on the brakes, it sounds like finger nails on a chalkboard. The driver's side window only goes one third of the way down. Only the radio works on the car stereo system.

She is planning to buy a used car. She has saved up $2,100 for the purchase. She figures she needs about $4,000 to get a good, reliable used vehicle.

But now, the transmission on her car starts failing. The car does not go in reverse. She must always park the car in a way where she can pull forward when she exits the parking spot.

As she is heading home from work one day, she is stopped at a red light, and she spies a used black and tan car at the dealership on the corner. The light turns green, and she steps on the accelerator, but the car stalls. Sherri has had enough!

She shakes her head and restarts the car. Instead of going home, she turns into the used car lot of the dealership. She is going to get a new used car.

Sherri checks out the black and tan car. The tires are great. The brake pedal does not go halfway to the floor, and there is no high-pitch squeal. The car's stereo system comes with a radio, CD player, and a place to plug in her MP3 player, and all of these components are functional. All of the electric windows go up and down all the way. Plus, the car goes both forward *and* backward.

She haggles over the price of the car. Total cost of the car will be $4,500 for everything.

She takes her credit card from her purse, and she gives it to the salesman. He asks if she would rather use their financing, but she declines.

She is going to use $2,100 from her savings, and she will pay off the $2,400 by making monthly payments of one hundred dollars to her credit card.

She has twenty-five days of interest-free financing with this credit card. Sherri wastes no time. She goes through the mail that has been piling up for the last one to two weeks. She finds the envelope that she is looking for.

It is a credit card offer with 0 percent financing for twelve months without an annual fee. This is what Sherri needs. She does not want to pay any interest whatsoever.

She reads the offer to make sure she understands the terms of the agreement. She fills out the application completely, signs it, and mails it.

She then goes online to her existing credit card company's website. She logs on to her account and makes a payment of $2,100. The balance on the credit card is now $2,400.

About two weeks later, Sherri receives her new credit card in the mail. She calls to activate the card and declines all of the credit protection services offered by the credit card's representative.

She sets it to use right away. Her rent, car insurance, new car registration, gas, electric, cable, and cell phone bills are payable now. She has the money to pay the bills, but she is going to use her new credit card instead. She charges all of the bills to her new credit card. She also charges her gasoline and groceries. Her total charges amount to $2,600.

She takes the money she was going to pay these bills with and instead makes a $2,400 payment to the old credit card. The old credit card's balance is now zero.

Sherri also makes a $300 payment to her new credit card: $200 is for the bills; one hundred dollars is her monthly payment on the new used car.

Sherri will no longer make any charges on her new credit card. She will make hundred-dollar monthly payments for the next eleven months.

Month	Payment	Balance
January	$100	$2,300
February	$100	$2,200
March	$100	$2,100
April	$100	$2,000
May	$100	$1,900
June	$100	$1,800
July	$100	$1,700
August	$100	$1,600
September	$100	$1,500
October	$100	$1,400
November	$100	$1,300
December	$1,300	$0

In November, Sherri responds to another credit card offering fifteen months 0 percent financing and no annual fee.

She receives the new credit card in the mail.

She charges $1,500 in monthly expenses to her new credit card.

Sherri makes a $1,300 payment to the old credit card. The balance is now zero.

Sherri also makes a $300 payment to the new credit card company: $200 is for the bills; one hundred dollars is her monthly payment on the car.

Sherri makes no other charges with this credit card. She will continue to make monthly payments of one hundred dollars for the next twelve months.

Month	Payment	Balance
December	$100	$1,200
January	$100	$1,100
February	$100	$1,000
March	$100	$900
April	$100	$800
May	$100	$700
June	$100	$600
July	$100	$500
August	$100	$400
September	$100	$300
October	$100	$200
November	$100	$100
December	$100	$0

No more debt for Sherri, and the car still runs great!

Summary

A lot of people are unaware that you can purchase a vehicle with a credit card. Dealerships do not bring this issue up at the negotiation table. Most people do not have big enough credit limits on their credit cards to qualify to purchase vehicles. The other reason is that the dealerships make money off consumers who finance with the dealership.

The dealer tried to talk Sherri into financing with his company, but Sherri would have none of it. She was never going to pay any interest. To Sherri, the concept of paying interest is silly.

She used three credit cards.

The first she used to purchase the vehicle.

Then she moved the balance of the first credit card to the second credit card without paying any balance transfer fees (that would be silly to Sherri also). She made hundred-dollar monthly payments for nearly twelve months, taking advantage of 0 percent financing.

Then Sherri moved the balance of the second credit card to a third credit card without paying a balance transfer fee. She continued to make one-hundred-dollar payments until the debt was erased.

Chapter 16

Erase a $1,000 Debt without Using Your Money

Allan's brakes squeak a little.

When Allan takes his car to the shop, he is shocked to find out that both sets of brakes and two rotors need to be replaced. He lets out a heavy sigh. He tells the mechanics to just do it. The work will cost Allan $1,000.

He knows he will be able to reduce the bill to $900 because the new credit card he carries comes with a hundred-dollar sign-up bonus after $1,000 in purchases. This is the $1,000 purchase.

He wonders to himself, "Can I do this nine more times and pay for the brakes?"

The credit card comes with 0 percent financing for fifteen months. "Maybe that will be long enough," he thinks to himself.

For the next month (January), Allan and his wife submit five credit card applications that have come in the mail. They each submit the applications under their own names. This way they can take advantage of two offers by the same credit card company. The total in sign-up bonuses could equal $600 (one $150 bonus after the first purchase, one $200 bonus after the first purchase, two hundred-dollar bonuses after $1,000 in purchases, and one fifty-dollar bonus after $500 in purchases).

In January, Allan does not have to make a payment to the credit card. He simply has the credit card company credit his account with the one-hundred-dollar sign-up bonus he earned by using the credit card to pay for his brake job. The balance on his credit card is now $900.

All five of Allan and his wife's credit cards applications are accepted. They first use the two credit cards that qualify for the sign-up bonus with a single purchase (the $150 sign-up bonus and the $200 sign-up bonus). Then they charge the other credit cards with their monthly expenses to reach the qualifying amounts. They pay off all five balances with the money they were going to use to pay their bills anyway.

In February, Allan makes a $350 payment to the credit card company he used to pay for his new brakes. The $350 is from the first two sign-up bonuses ($150 and $200). Allan now cancels both of those credit cards and cuts them up. The new balance on his credit card is now $550.

In March, Allan receives two of the three remaining sign-up bonuses. He gets one of the hundred-dollar bonuses and the fifty-dollar bonus. He then cancels those two credit cards and cuts them up.

He makes a $150 payment on the credit card that he used to pay for his brake job. The new balance on the credit card is now $400.

Also in March, Allan and his wife respond to two more credit card solicitations each offering a hundred-dollar bonus. One credit card requires $1,000 in purchases, and the other credit card requires $500 in purchases.

In April Allan receives the other hundred-dollar bonus. He cancels this credit card and cuts it up. He makes a payment of one hundred dollars to the credit card that he used to pay for his new brakes and rotors. The new balance on the credit card is $300.

Allan and his wife receive the two new credit cards they had applied for back in March. They each come with a hundred-dollar sign-up bonus. They activate the credit cards and charge the qualifying amounts to the credit cards. They pay the balances off as soon as they are credited on their respective credit card company websites.

Another credit card offer comes in the mail this month. This credit card offers a $150 sign-up bonus after $1,000 in qualifying purchases. Allan applies for it.

In May, Allan receives one of the hundred-dollar bonuses. He calls up that credit card company and cancels the account. He then cuts up the credit card.

He makes a hundred-dollar payment on the credit card he used for his brake job. The new credit card balance is now $200.

In June, Allan receives both of the remaining sign-up bonuses totaling $250. He calls both of the credit card companies and cancels both accounts. He cuts up both cards.

He makes his last payment ($200) to the credit card company he owes. The debt is erased.

The brakes and rotors were paid for by someone else.

With the extra fifty dollars, Allan and his wife go out to dinner to celebrate!

Summary

Allan had a $1,000 debt.

Like most people, Allan did not want to pay for it. He used other people's money: the sign-up bonuses offered by the credit card companies.

Allan used nine credit cards to eliminate a $1,000 debt.

He made $6,000 in charges. The first $1,000 was the brake job. The other $5,000 were charges in monthly expenses such as car insurance, utilities, phone, gasoline, and groceries. He was going to pay these with his debit card online, but instead he used the credit cards. Then he paid the credit cards off with his checking account immediately so as to incur no interest charges.

He received nine sign-up bonuses.

1. After $1,000 in charges: $100
2. After first purchase: $150
3. After first purchase: $200
4. After $1,000 in charges: $100
5. After $500 in charges: $50
6. After $1,000 in charges: $100
7. After $1000 in charges: $100
8. After $500 in charges: $100
9. After $1,000 in charges: $150

Allan received $1,050 in sign-up bonuses. He cleared an extra fifty dollars—not a bad deal for Allan.

Chapter 17

Questions and Answers

Q: I have an annual fee on my credit card. The annual fee is waived for the first year. If I close the account before the annual fee becomes due, do I have to pay back the sign-up and cash-back bonuses I have received?

A: No.

The annual fee is part of the terms of the credit card agreement you signed up for. The credit card company waives the fee for the first year. This is part of the agreement. So, you are free to cancel at any time and keep any rewards the credit card company has paid to you.

Q: Should I have my bills set up as automatic payments on my credit card?

A: No.

You need to control *what* you put on your credit card and *when* you charge something on your credit card.

It is easy to forget an automatic payment. Enough time may elapse before you realize you have a charge on your credit card, and you might end up paying a finance charge. Even worse, you might end up paying a late fee. A late fee is even more of a waste of money than paying an interest charge. Do not sign up for automatic payments.

Q: How do you keep track of your credit card charges?

A: This is an often-asked question.

I keep track of my credit card charges in a notebook. Every year around August, school supplies are cheaper. The prices of notebooks are sometimes a quarter or even a dime. I get a couple of notebooks at a time.

I use the notebook in the same way I would a checkbook register.

Just as you write every debit from your checking account in your register, I do the same, but in a notebook. Here is an example:

Groceries	$497.34
Gasoline	$352.00
Power	$287.56
Gas	$46.23
Water	$27.15
Car Insurance	$157.29
Misc.	<u>$137.65</u>
Total	$1,505.22

Credit card payment = $1,505.22

My checkbook register will only have one debit entry for the credit card payment.

So basically, all I am doing is writing down the bills I pay in a notebook instead of cluttering up a checkbook register. My checkbook register lasts a long time.

Q: Will I hurt my credit rating by opening and closing credit card accounts?

A: I have not found this to be the case. As you know, I often open and close credit card accounts. I have never been denied for a credit card since my early twenties.

Many so-called experts have said that closing your credit card accounts can be detrimental due to the fact that you have less credit available. This would not be the case when you close one credit card account and open up another credit card account. You will also probably notice that every major credit card you receive will have about the same credit limit available. So the similarity in credit limits would negate the availability-of-credit argument.

Q: Do you keep any credit card for a long period of time?

A: Yes.

Just like Tom from chapter 9, I have one credit card that I have kept through the years. This one comes with a cash-back bonus. It comes with periodic promotional increases in the cash-back percentage. Every year around those three months, I use this credit card.

Q: Have you really just made one purchase like Ralph from chapter 2, and then collected a $150 check?

A: Yes.

I have done this several times with varying amounts. The two most common amounts have been a hundred-dollar sign-up bonus and a $150 sign-up bonus after one purchase.

After I receive the bonuses and the checks have cleared the bank, I cancel the credit cards and cut them up.

Q: Don't you feel guilty about doing this?

A: No.

This is a business agreement between two parties. After both parties have fulfilled their obligations, there is no need for a relationship.

But always remember this: if you don't feel comfortable doing something, then don't do it.

Q: Aren't you encouraging people to go into debt?

A: No.

It is stated in the first chapter of this book. If you do not have the money to pay off the credit card, then do not use it. The four rules are listed here again.

1. Never pay any interest.
2. Never apply for a credit card with an annual fee.
3. Never pay a balance-transfer fee.
4. Have the money first, charge the card, and then pay the card.

Q: What's wrong with an annual fee? My annual fee is $175 a year, and I get great benefits with the credit card.

A: If you are happy with your credit card, then keep it.

The annual fee is just detrimental to your cash-back bonus accumulation. For example, if your credit card comes with a 2 percent cash-back bonus, it will take $8,750 in credit card charges to break even ($8,750 × 2 percent = $175, the annual fee).

It is worse if your credit card offers only a 1 percent cash-back bonus. It will take $17,500 in credit card charges to break even because of the $175 annual fee.

If you are charging $10,000 or more a month, then the annual fee would make sense as long as the credit card comes with a 2 percent or more in cash-back bonuses. In the following examples, you would have charged $120,000 for the year.

Without an annual fee at a 1 percent cash-back bonus rate, the credit card user would earn $1,200.

With an annual fee of $175 at a 1 percent cash-back bonus rate, the credit card user would earn $1,025.

With an annual fee of $175 at a 2 percent cash-back bonus rate, the credit card user would earn $2,225.

So for the annual fee to make financial sense, the cash-back bonus rate needs to be 2 percent or more on all purchases. The credit card user would also have to charge a lot more on his credit card to not only break even but to come out ahead.

Charging $10,000 or more on a credit card every month and paying it off does not work for the average American household. The average household makes much less than $120,000 a year.

It is best to stay clear of annual fees. Always remember to do the simple math.

Q: Isn't it a hassle to call credit card companies to cancel all those credit cards?

A: Sometimes yes.

It costs the credit card company money to process an account, and they want to make money off you and the merchants.

Usually the credit card representative will ask you why you are canceling the account. I usually respond, "I have too many credit cards at this time." Then the representative usually points out all the great benefits that come with the credit card.

Sometimes the representative will offer an additional cash bonus like they did for Granny back in chapter 12. If the cash bonus is easy to achieve, I keep the credit card. As soon as I earn the cash bonus, I cancel and cut up the credit card.

Sometimes the representative will offer 0 percent financing for a certain length of time as way to keep my business. This is more common way to try and retain me than a cash bonus.

I always find the offering of the 0 percent financing funny. The representatives usually speak very kindly and gently. They will offer me six months of 0 percent financing. They go on to say that I can transfer a balance from another credit card that I am now paying interest on. There will be a balance-transfer fee, but my savings could be substantial by not paying any interest (or so they tell me!). I just chuckle to myself.

I believe the representative has no clue that you can transfer a balance to any credit card without paying a balance-transfer fee. If he did know this, he probably could not tell you since this would cost the credit card company money.

I always kindly refuse the 0 percent financing they offer.

Q: Why not try to get airplane miles?

A: The ideas espoused in this book can be used to cash in airline miles; however the process takes longer.

Human beings like instant gratification. Unfortunately, instant gratification is not involved with making money with credit cards. But it is a lot quicker to cash in a hundred-dollar cash bonus and see the results of your work in three to six weeks than to wait six-plus months or more to acquire enough points to cash in an airplane ticket. Sometimes there are restrictions as to when the airline ticket can be used (blackout dates, for example). When you take a cash bonus, it is yours to do with as you please. It is freedom!

Q: How did you learn to make money with credit cards?

A: The first idea came to me in the 1990s.

Back then, the credit card companies would send you blank checks like they do today; but unlike today, they would not charge you a balance transfer fee to use their checks. (Today it can cost you anywhere from 3 to 5 percent of the balance.) The check would also come with 0 percent financing. Let us say for our example that the 0 percent financing is for nine months.

I would write a $6,500 check at the bank. The bank teller would give me a judgmental look. (The look said, "Don't you know using the credit card like this is a stupid idea?" Sometimes a teller would verbalize a comment like that.)

I would then open up a $5,000 certificate of deposit for six months. In the 1990s, I could get a CD rate of 4 percent to 5 percent. For this example, I got the CD for 5 percent.

The other $1,500 would go into the savings account. Interest rates on savings accounts were better back then too. For the next five months, each month I would transfer $300 from my savings account to my checking account. Each month for five months I would make a $300 payment to the credit card company. I would pay them with their own money.

The sixth month I would cash out my certificate of deposit which by then would be worth $5,125. I would send in $5,000 as a final payment to the credit card company, making the credit card balance zero. I had earned $125 plus whatever interest I made off the savings account.

Six months later, the same credit card company would offer the same promotion, and I would go through the process all over again. I knew I was onto something.

Eventually the credit card companies started charging to use the checks. And the certificate of deposit and savings account rates plummeted. That was the end of an era.

Now we are in the cash-back bonus era. Some credit cards are now offering 2 or 3 percent cash-back bonuses permanently. Unfortunately most of those credit cards come with an annual fee. If the annual fee is $150 with a 2 percent cash-back bonus, you have to charge $7,500 before you are in the black. That sucks!

EPILOGUE

The cost to publish this book was about $800. I used a POD (print-on-demand) company. I paid the publishing costs for this book with money I received from three credit card companies.

During or before the writing of this book, I started using a new credit card. This credit card came with a cash-back bonus program with various promotional items on varying cash-back percentages. It also offered a 25 percent bonus when I cashed in any cash-back bonus of $300 or more. I cashed out $425 plus the 25 percent bonus of $106.50 for a total of $531.25.

The next card I used came with a $150 sign-up bonus after one qualifying purchase. I used this credit card for my retreat to Pioche, Nevada, to finish this book. The total amount of the check sent to me was $152.76.

On the last card I used, I earned a $150 sign-up bonus after $1,000 in qualifying purchases. After I charged a little over the qualifying amount, I requested to have the $150 sign-up bonus deposited in my checking account. About three days later, my checking account was credited with the $150. This credit card was in my wife's name. She called the credit card company and canceled the account. I cut up the credit card.

Three credit cards paid for the publishing costs of this book. There were no out-of-pocket expenses for me.

Now it is your turn to earn some extra cash! It is time to start cashing in on credit cards! Make money by paying your bills!